POCKET INTERNATIONAL BUSINESS TERMS

OTHER TITLES FROM
THE ECONOMIST BOOKS

The Economist Desk Companion
The Economist Guide to Economic Indicators
The Economist Guide to the European Union
The Economist Numbers Guide
The Economist Style Guide
The Dictionary of Economics
The International Dictionary of Finance
Going Digital
Improving Marketing Effectiveness
Management Development
Measuring Business Performance

Pocket Accounting
Pocket Advertising
Pocket Director
Pocket Employer
Pocket Finance
Pocket Information Technology
Pocket Investor
Pocket Law
Pocket Manager
Pocket Marketing
Pocket MBA
Pocket Negotiator
Pocket Strategy
Pocket Telecommunications

The Economist Pocket Asia
The Economist Pocket Europe in Figures
The Economist Pocket World in Figures

The Economist Books

POCKET INTERNATIONAL BUSINESS TERMS

TIM HINDLE

THE ECONOMIST IN ASSOCIATION WITH
PROFILE BOOKS LTD

Profile Books Ltd
58A Hatton Garden, London EC1N 8LX

Published by Profile Books Ltd
in association with
The Economist Newspaper Ltd 1999

Printed in Italy by
LEGO S.p.a. – Vicenza – Italy

A CIP catalogue record for this book is available
from the British Library

ISBN 1 86197 180 X

Introduction

International Business Terms is one in a series of books that brings the clarity for which *The Economist* is famous to the often confusing subject of business. It is written by Tim Hindle, a former business editor, management editor and finance editor of *The Economist.*

The A–Z contains more than 1,500 terms which are widely used by people working in business and commerce around the world.

Words in small capitals usually indicate a separate entry, thus enabling readers to find other relevant information (although they should note abbreviations, such as EU and CD, are also in small capitals).

This pocket series is designed to take the mystique out of business and financial jargon in a stimulating and entertaining way.

Other titles in the series are:

Pocket Accounting
Pocket Advertising
Pocket Director
Pocket Employer
Pocket Finance
Pocket Information Technology
Pocket Investor
Pocket Law
Pocket Manager
Pocket Marketing
Pocket MBA
Pocket Negotiator
Pocket Strategy
Pocket Telecommunications

AAA
Triple A, the highest classification that an individual ISSUE of DEBT can receive from a CREDIT-RATING AGENCY. It is used to describe things like American government bonds or the bonds of companies with the best pedigree. More generally, AAA means first class.

A AND B SHARES
In countries such as the United States and the UK, almost all shares in a PUBLIC COMPANY have equal rights. But in some countries, such as Sweden, companies can issue two different kinds of shares, A and B shares. B shares are frequently issued to members of a FIRM's founding family, and each one has the same VOTING RIGHTS as several A shares. A and B shares inevitably have a different market value, although it is surprising what a small value investors put on voting rights.

ABOVE THE LINE
An expression used in accounting to refer to those INCOME and expenditure items in a PROFIT AND LOSS ACCOUNT that appear above the NET PROFIT figure. The expression is also used in MARKETING to refer to that part of the marketing BUDGET that is spent on ADVERTISING in the MEDIA. Other forms of marketing activity, such as SALES PROMOTION or DIRECT MARKETING, are referred to as BELOW THE LINE.

ABSENTEEISM
The percentage of a COMPANY'S WORKFORCE that is absent on any given working day. Levels of absenteeism vary with:

- the seasons;
- the stress to which the workforce is subjected; and
- the conditions in the workplace.

ABSTENTION
The deliberate refusal to cast a vote, particularly on the part of a DIRECTOR in a COMPANY'S BOARD MEETING. An abstention is recorded as a vote that is

neither in favour of nor against the matter under discussion.

ACCELERATED DEPRECIATION
A method of DEPRECIATION that, for the purposes of company ACCOUNTS, allows larger sums to be written off the VALUE of assets in their earlier years than in their later years. In the alternative STRAIGHT-LINE method of depreciation, equal amounts are written off the ASSET each year.

ACCEPTANCE
A BILL OF EXCHANGE (or BANK DRAFT) that has been accepted by a BANK; that is, the bank has given its guarantee that it will honour the bill should the BUYER of the GOODS fail to do so.

ACCOUNT
The record of an amount of MONEY that has been deposited with (or borrowed from) a FINANCIAL INSTITUTION (most commonly a BANK, as in bank account). The payment that a bank makes for having the use of such money over time is called INTEREST.

There are a number of different types of accounts, each paying a different RATE OF INTEREST. In general, the rate depends on:

- how long depositors are prepared to leave their money in the account; and
- how much notice they agree to give before withdrawing it.

ACCOUNT DIRECTOR
A person within an ADVERTISING AGENCY who manages the agency's relationship with its clients. Account directors lead the teams of people who put together a CAMPAIGN and are the main point of contact for clients.

ACCOUNTANT
An individual who works on the preparation of ACCOUNTS. An accountant may be employed by a COMPANY to work on its internal accounts, or by an independent FIRM of accountants to AUDIT the

records of a number of different companies. Those who do accounting work may be qualified or unqualified, but in most countries the person with the ultimate responsibility for auditing a company's accounts must have passed relevant accounting exams.

Accounting period

The period of time covered by a COMPANY's published PROFIT AND LOSS ACCOUNT. This is usually (but not necessarily) a 12-month period.

Accounting principles

Accountants follow a number of principles that act as guidelines whenever there is controversy over the way to treat items in a COMPANY'S ACCOUNTS. The principles are that:

- things should be **consistent** – that is, if in doubt do what you did last time;
- things should **match** – that is, revenue and expenses should be attributed to the period in which they arose, and not to the period when they were actually received or paid;
- it should be assumed that the business is a **going concern**; and
- **prudence** should be applied at all times.

Accounting standards

Although a COMPANY'S ACCOUNTS attempt to measure precisely its performance, there are a number of different ways of measuring some of the items in those accounts. Accounting standards are issued by the accounting profession to recommend a best practice for the treatment of controversial items.

Accounts

The financial records of a COMPANY's transactions kept according to the principles of DOUBLE-ENTRY BOOK-KEEPING. For every debit there is an equal and opposite credit. There are a number of different types of accounts.

- **Annual accounts.** The financial statements that have to be presented to shareholders every year by law. These usually consist of a balance sheet, a profit and loss account and a statement from the chairman on the current state of play.
- **Consolidated accounts.** The accounts of a GROUP of companies, in which inter-company transactions are netted out.
- **Interim accounts.** Accounts for periods of less than a year. Interim accounts usually cover six months and appear mid-way between the annual accounts.

(See also MANAGEMENT ACCOUNTS.)

ACCOUNTS PAYABLE
A record of the amounts of MONEY that an ORGANISATION owes, and of the dates when it owes them.

ACCOUNTS RECEIVABLE
A record of the amounts of MONEY that are owed to an ORGANISATION, and of the dates on which they are due.

ACCRUAL
In accounting, the recognition of events as and when they take place – as opposed to when the CASH paid for them actually changes hands.

ACCRUED INTEREST
INTEREST that has been earned but not yet paid. If interest on a BANK DEPOSIT is paid every six months, then five months after the last payment five-sixths of the next interest payment can be said to have accrued. None of it, however, will be paid for another month.

ACID TEST
The ratio of a COMPANY'S SHORT-TERM liabilities (for example, its ACCOUNTS PAYABLE, and its INTEREST and DEBT repayments) to its short-term assets (for example, CASH in the BANK and easily marketable securities). The acid test is also called the QUICK

RATIO and provides a rough guide of a company's LIQUIDITY.

ACQUISITION
The purchase by one COMPANY of a controlling interest in another; an alternative to organic growth for any company in a hurry to become bigger. Acquisitions can be friendly – when both companies reach agreement about a deal and it is called a MERGER – or hostile, when some shareholders and/or the MANAGEMENT resist the attempt to buy them. (See also M&A.)

ACTION
French for SHARE, and the stem for a whole range of related words, for example, *actionnaire* (SHAREHOLDER).

ACTUARY
A person who calculates the RISK associated with various kinds of LONG-TERM INSURANCE policies. In particular, an actuary calculates the probability that someone of a specific age and profile will die within a given period of time. Actuaries are disparagingly said to be people who find accounting too exciting.

ADDED VALUE
The concept behind value added tax (VAT); the idea that VALUE is added to GOODS and SERVICES at many discrete stages during their production. VAT seeks to tax that value at each of those stages.

ADDENDUM
Something that is added to a CONTRACT as an afterthought.

ADJOURNMENT
The brief postponement of a MEETING in midstream. A BOARD MEETING, for example, might be adjourned for lunch. If an adjournment lasts longer than a few hours, the meeting has to be brought to a proper close and reconvened at another time.

Adjustable rate
A rate of interest on a loan that varies according to market rates. As market rates go up and down so does an adjustable rate, but usually with a time lag.

Adjuster
A person employed by an insurance company to assess the amounts that have been claimed by the holder of an insurance policy to have been lost or damaged. The idea is that the adjuster (also known as a loss adjuster) evaluates the claims of the policyholders and makes recommendations to the insurer as to how those claims should be adjusted.

Administration
A legal process in the UK whereby a hard-pressed company can gain time in which to try and settle its debts. It is similar to chapter 11 in the United States and *vergleich* in Germany. The company's directors apply to the courts to appoint an administrator (usually an accountant) who tries to arrange a deal between the company and its creditors. Any such deal should:

- allow the company to carry on trading; and
- repay the creditors a satisfactory percentage of what they are owed.

Administrator
Someone appointed by a court to run a company that is under administration. Also someone appointed by a court to handle a dead person's affairs when there is no will, or when the executors appointed by the will are unable to carry out their responsibilities.

ADR
Short for American depositary receipt, a certificate issued by an American bank to an American investor in lieu of a foreign security. ADRs are traded in the United States as if they were domestic stock. In particular, the issuer (the bank) arranges for the dividends to be paid in dollars.

Ad valorem
Something (such as a tax) that is based on the value of goods and not on their quantity. Thus vat is an ad valorem tax; so too is sales tax in the United States. A fixed-sum tax levied on the owner of a car is not since it bears no relation to the value of the car or the use that it makes of the roads.

Advance
An amount of money that is paid in advance. For example, cash given to an employee for his or her travel expenses before the expenses are incurred. Owners of intellectual copyright (such as authors) are often paid an advance against future royalties that they earn on sales of their work.

Advertisement
An announcement of the merits of a product or service. The announcement can appear in a variety of media: newspapers and magazines; television and cinema; billboards and other outside sites; internet web sites; and so on. An organisation placing an advertisement in the media pays for the privilege.

Advertising
The business of preparing and placing advertisements in the media.

Half the money I spend on advertising is wasted, and the trouble is I don't know which half.
Attributed to Lord Leverhulme in the UK and to Sam Wannamaker in the United States

Advertising agency
A company that specialises in designing and producing advertisements for other organisations. It may also take on the task of deciding where to show the advertisements that it produces, and when.

Advisory board
A committee without formal power set up by a

COMPANY'S BOARD to advise its directors on specific subjects. For example, a company may have an international advisory board consisting of people of different nationalities and cultures. Their role is to offer advice on INVESTMENT and markets in the parts of the world with which they are familiar.

Affidavit
A sworn statement made in front of a person authorised by the courts to witness statements made under oath.

Affiliate
A COMPANY that is partly owned by another company. Non-corporate entities that have close links with each other are also sometimes said to be affiliates. Individual trade unions, for instance, are affiliated to their central ORGANISATION. (See also SUBSIDIARY and ASSOCIATE.)

Affirmative action
A corporate policy designed to rectify previous inequalities. For example, affirmative action in the recruitment of women or people from racial minorities involves hiring more employees from these groups than would have occurred in the normal course of events.

AG
Short for Aktiengesellschaft, a German form of corporation.

Agenda
A written list of the items to be discussed at a MEETING. An agenda is prepared before the meeting and is circulated in advance to all those who are attending. The last item is normally "any other business", which provides those attending with an opportunity to raise unanticipated issues.

Agent
Someone who acts on behalf of somebody else, the principal, and with the principal's agreement. The important part of the agency relationship is

the extent of authority granted by the principal to the agent. Full authority means that the agent has the power to enter into a CONTRACT on behalf of the principal and to bind it contractually without its further involvement. In contrast, a principal may authorise its agent to procure orders in such a way that the principal reserves the right to accept or decline the orders – and thus decides for itself whether to accept a binding contract. Where an agent sells goods on behalf of a principal, such as a REAL ESTATE agent (realtor), the agent never acquires TITLE to the GOODS or property. When a contract for the SALE of something is concluded, title passes directly from the principal to the BUYER. This distinguishes an agency from a distributorship. A distributor buys the goods from the SUPPLIER, acquires title to them, and resells them on its own account, thereby itself acting as a principal.

AGM

Short for annual general meeting, a MEETING held once a year in which a COMPANY's managers report to its shareholders on the company's performance during the year. Among the regular events at an AGM are an announcement of the DIVIDEND payment and a vote by the shareholders on whether to retain the same auditors.

AIR RIGHTS

The rights to the air above existing buildings. In large cities, where there is a possibility of building skyscrapers in built-up areas, air rights can be extremely valuable.

AIR WAYBILL

A document that lists GOODS that are to be transported internationally by a shipper. The air waybill constitutes an agreement between the shipper and the owner of the goods that the goods will be delivered to an agreed destination in the same condition in which they were received.

AIR FREIGHT

The transport of the GOODS by air. Air freight is invariably more expensive than transport by sea or land, but it is far quicker. It is much used, therefore, for transporting perishable goods.

ALLIANCE
The linking of two or more organisations for their mutual benefit. The nature of the link can range from a loose special relationship with a preferred SUPPLIER to a full-blown EQUITY stake. Companies form alliances for a number of reasons, one of which is to reduce the risk of entering new markets or of developing new products by themselves.

ALLOTMENT
The amount of STOCK that is allocated to investors who have subscribed for a new ISSUE of shares.

ALL RISK
An INSURANCE policy that covers all risks except for those specifically stated in the policy.

ALPHA STOCK
The most actively traded stocks on the London STOCK EXCHANGE. A continuous two-way MARKET in all alpha stocks is guaranteed by the market-makers on the exchange.

ALTERNATE
Someone who is officially named as the stand-by should a particular OFFICE-holder not be able to carry out his or her duties. For instance, a COMPANY may appoint a number of people to its BOARD as alternate directors. This is appropriate if the directors are absent a lot and unable to attend regular board meetings. Alternates have all the powers of the office-holders for whom they stand in.

ALTERNATIVE INVESTMENT
Investments other than securities and MONEY, such as works of art, coins, stamps, gems and gold.

AMENDMENT
An alteration or an addition to a legal document

that is signed by all the parties to the document. The amendment has the same legal status as the rest of the document.

AMORTISATION
The preferred word in the United States for DEPRECIATION.

ANALYST
A person employed to analyse something. In the BUSINESS world there are two main types of analysts:

- An INVESTMENT analyst is someone who analyses the performance of companies and their SHARE PRICE for the benefit of investors.
- A systems analyst is someone who designs computer systems and looks for ways in which they can be improved.

ANNUAL REPORT
The printed document that contains the annual ACCOUNTS of a COMPANY. The annual report is posted to all shareholders every year. The quality of companies' annual reports varies greatly.

ANNUITY
An INVESTMENT that yields a fixed annual INCOME for the INVESTOR until his or her death. The payment of an annuity used to be annual, but it is now frequently more frequent.

ANTI-DUMPING
See DUMPING.

ANTI-TRUST
Laws in the United States which make it illegal for firms to fix prices among themselves or to discriminate in the prices that they ask different buyers for the same GOODS. The same body of legislation makes it illegal for companies to form a MONOPOLY.

APPRAISAL
A formal process of assessing the performance of

an individual EMPLOYEE on a regular basis, usually annually. The aim is not only to discuss the employee's past performance but also to consider his or her aims and TRAINING needs. See also INVESTMENT APPRAISAL.

APPRECIATION

The increase in the VALUE of an ASSET over time; the opposite of DEPRECIATION. There are not many assets on a company's BALANCE SHEET that appreciate, but some do. The value of a PATENT, for instance, might well appreciate as the market potential of the patented PRODUCT increases. Likewise, if the company has a policy of putting a value on its BRANDS, it will be hoping to increase their value.

APPRENTICE

A person who learns a TRADE or skill on the job, and whose teacher is someone who is already a master of that skill. Formal apprenticeship schemes existed as long ago as the Middle Ages.

APPROPRIATION

MONEY that is set aside for a specific purpose. A COMPANY's appropriation account presents a statement of the payments that the company is already committed to in the future (and for what purpose) and of where the money to make the payments is to come from.

APR

Short for annualised percentage rate, a standardised way of expressing annual rates of INTEREST. The APR enables consumers to make a direct comparison between the COST of one form of CREDIT and another. The formula for calculating APR is as follows. Where:

x is the rate of interest quoted for a period less than a year and y is the number of such periods in a year, then

$$\text{APR} = 100 \times [(1 + x/100)^y - 1]$$

Arbitrage
The buying and selling of goods or SERVICES on different markets to take advantage of variations in PRICE. People who make their living by arbitrage are called arbitrageurs.

Arbitration
A procedure for solving commercial disputes that avoids going to court. The parties to the dispute turn to an independent THIRD PARTY whose judgment they agree in advance to accept. A number of industries have set up special international bodies for the purpose of arbitrating in disputes within their INDUSTRY.

Arbitrator
A person who acts as an intermediary in a case of ARBITRATION; an independent THIRD PARTY whose opinion the disputing parties agree to be bound by. In some cases the arbitrator may consist of a panel of individuals.

Arm's length
A transaction between entirely independent parties, each of whom acts only in his or her best interest.

Arrears
The making of a regular payment (of RENT or INTEREST, for example) after the period to which it relates.

Articles of association
The set of rules by which a COMPANY is run. The articles state, for instance, what percentage of the shareholders are required to vote in favour of major changes before they can be put into effect. Such changes frequently require more than a simple majority. The articles of association are lodged with the relevant authority at the time when a company is first registered. As such, they become a part of the public record.

Assembly line
A method of production in which workers sit or stand in front of a moving conveyor belt on which is carried an unfinished PRODUCT. The workers carry out precisely the same task on each product. This form of production was pioneered by the Ford Motor Company.

Asset
Something that a COMPANY or individual owns to which can be ascribed a VALUE, from plant to patents, and from property to products. (See also CURRENT ASSET, FIXED ASSET and INTANGIBLE ASSET.)

Asset management
The business of managing assets to make them produce maximum REVENUE over the longer term. The expression is generally used in the context of financial assets.

Asset stripping
A process in which a COMPANY or an individual buys an ASSET (frequently a QUOTED COMPANY) and then proceeds to sell it bit by bit. Asset stripping is most common when the STOCKMARKET's valuation of the whole of a BUSINESS is less than the sum of its parts.

Assign
To record the transfer of the ownership of an ASSET from one person to another. Some contracts impose restrictions on the assignment of their benefits and obligations.

Associated
COMPANY A is an associated company of company B if more than 20%, but less than 50%, of its EQUITY is owned by company B. Associated companies have to be consolidated into the ACCOUNTS of the company that owns the equity stake only if that company also controls the composition of the BOARD of the associated company.

Assurance
Usually referred to as life assurance, a form of INSURANCE against the risk of something which is assured of happening, such as death. The insurer agrees to pay a lump sum should the insured person die within a stated period. Some policies are a form of savings scheme in which the insurer pays for an agreed income stream in the future in return for regular payments in the present.

ATM
Short for automated teller machine, an electronic machine that carries out a number of the functions of a BANK teller: handing out CASH, producing bank statements, and so on. ATMS are most frequently found on the outside walls of bank branches.

Auction
A systematic process for selling something (REAL ESTATE, paintings, fish, and so on) to the highest bidder from among several potential buyers. (See also DUTCH AUCTION.)

Audit
The regular and systematic process of checking that a COMPANY'S ACCOUNTS are TRUE AND FAIR. The audit is carried out by an independent ACCOUNTANT from a FIRM that has an ARM'S LENGTH relationship with the company whose accounts it is auditing. The word comes from the Latin *auditus*, meaning hearing. In olden times it referred to the hearing that landowners gave to the manager of their land (urban or agricultural), while the manager accounted for his stewardship.

Audit committee
The subcommittee of a COMPANY'S BOARD, to which is delegated the responsibility for choosing the company's auditors and for negotiating their FEE. Audit committees are required of companies seeking to be listed on the New York Stock Exchange.

Audit trail
The route by which an AUDITOR checks back from

a particular item in the ACCOUNTS to the activity that gave rise to the item (and the person who authorised the activity).

AUDITOR
The person who carries out the AUDIT of a COMPANY'S ACCOUNTS.

AUTHORISED
The shares that a COMPANY is legally permitted to issue under the terms of its ARTICLES OF ASSOCIATION. A company may issue fewer shares if it wishes, but it may not issue more without first changing its articles.

AUTOMATION
The process of replacing human LABOUR with machines. The Luddites, a group of workers in 19th-century England, deliberately set out to destroy FACTORY machines on the ground that they would take away their livelihood.

AVERAGE COST
The total COST of producing GOODS (or of providing SERVICES) divided by the number of units produced or provided.

AVERAGE DAILY BALANCE
A method which banks use to calculate the INTEREST owing on a customer's account. They take the amounts outstanding on the account at the end of each working day of the month, add them together, and then divide by the number of days in the month. The interest owing is then calculated by multiplying the average daily balance by the monthly rate.

AWARD
A decision made by an ARBITRATOR in an ARBITRATION dispute. The award need not necessarily involve the exchange of MONEY. It may involve redefining boundaries between different property, for instance.

Baby boomer
A much-loved classification of consumers, consisting of people born between 1945 and 1965 in the United States and Europe. Being born in the aftermath of the second world war and being raised during the liberal years of the 1960s are believed to have given these people common characteristics as consumers.

Back-to-back
An importer that wishes to establish its creditworthiness with an exporter from another country can set up a BANK ACCOUNT in the exporter's country and place FUNDS in that account. Such funds act as COLLATERAL for GOODS that the importer subsequently buys from the exporter. They are referred to as a back-to-back facility.

Back office
A BUSINESS's behind-the-scenes operations. In financial institutions it is the people who sort out the paperwork; in manufacturing operations it is the people who make the paperwork.

Back pay
A SALARY or WAGE that is unpaid from a previous period. For weekly paid workers it is PAY due from the week before last; for monthly paid workers it is pay due for work done in the month before last.

Bad debt
A BILL or LOAN that is not paid within a reasonable period of time after its due-by date. Such late payments are described as doubtful debts for a while, but eventually they become bad debts. When that happens they have to be written off in the BUSINESS's ACCOUNTS (see WRITE OFF).

Balance
The difference between the credit and debit items in an ACCOUNT. If the credit items exceed the debit ones, the account is said to have a credit balance. If they do not, the account is said to be overdrawn.

BALANCE OF PAYMENTS
The record of a country's transactions with the rest of the world. The CURRENT ACCOUNT of the balance of payments consists of VISIBLE TRADE in GOODS; invisible trade in SERVICES; private transfer payments, such as MONEY sent home by nationals working abroad; and official transfers, such as payments to international organisations.

The CAPITAL account consists of LONG-TERM and SHORT-TERM transactions relating to a country's assets and liabilities (for example, loans and borrowings). Adding the current to the capital account gives the overall BALANCE, which should be matched by net monetary movements and changes in RESERVES. In practice, the data recorded never add up as they should in theory, and the gap is filled by an item called "errors and omissions".

BALANCE OF TRADE
A statement of a country's trading account with the rest of the world. This covers the import and export of GOODS and SERVICES.

BALANCE SHEET
The part of a COMPANY'S ACCOUNTS which lists its assets and liabilities. Fundamental to all such accounts is the idea that assets and liabilities are in BALANCE, that is, they are equal. The balance sheet is, of course, a snapshot of a company's position. A short time after it is compiled that position can, and sometimes does, change significantly.

BALLOON PAYMENT
The final payment on a LOAN that is being repaid in instalments. A balloon payment exceeds by some considerable amount the preceding payments. The repayments balloon as the MATURITY of the loan draws nigh.

BANK
A FINANCIAL INSTITUTION that carries out three basic functions:

- collects deposits from savers;

- makes loans to borrowers; and
- enables MONEY to be transmitted from one bank ACCOUNT to another by means of cheques, standing orders, direct debits, and so on.

There are a number of specialised banks that carry out particular functions. For example, a CENTRAL BANK acts as banker of last resort to the banking system; an INVESTMENT BANK is concerned with advising companies on how to raise money in the CAPITAL MARKET; and a clearing bank is the core of a country's money transmission system.

Banks are dinosaurs. Give me a piece of the transaction business, and they're history.
Bill Gates, co-founder of Microsoft

BANK CHARGES
The fees charged by banks for their services, such as MONEY transmission (clearing cheques and so on), CURRENCY conversion and arranging loans.

BANK DRAFT
An ORDER from a seller (or exporter) requesting the BANK of the buyer (or importer) to pay to the seller a specified amount. A sight draft is payable on presentation; a time draft is payable at a named future date. A bank draft is also known as a BILL OF EXCHANGE.

Capitalism without bankruptcy is like Christianity without hell.
Frank Borman, American astronaut

BANKRUPTCY
Being formally declared by a court unable to repay debts. A person who has been declared bankrupt is deprived of certain powers; for example, he or she cannot be a DIRECTOR of a COMPANY for a number of years. A bankrupt's assets are taken over by a TRUSTEE who distributes them among the unpaid creditors. (See also DISCHARGE.)

BAR CHART
A diagram consisting of a number of vertical bars placed next to each other. For example, a chart showing the number of cars sold by a dealer each month might have the number of cars plotted along the vertical axis and the months of the year along the horizontal axis.

BAR CODE
A rectangle of vertical black lines of varying thickness displayed on the side of CONSUMER GOODS. The lines are read by a laser beam which records electronically the PRODUCT's details, such as its PRICE, size, model number, and so on.

BARGAIN
There are two business-related meanings:

- Used as a noun, a bargain is a deal done at a PRICE below the acknowledged market price.
- Used as a verb, it refers to the process whereby a buyer and a seller reach agreement on a price.

BARRIER TO ENTRY
The obstacles that a COMPANY entering a MARKET for the first time has to surmount to thrive in that market. These include things like a shortage of suitable sites (for retailing), the absence of ECONOMIES OF SCALE (for MASS MARKET GOODS), and government regulations that protect domestic producers (for imports).

BARRIER TO EXIT
The obstacles that prevent a COMPANY leaving a MARKET when it no longer sees a prospect of making MONEY in that market. These include things like the COST of laying off STAFF and of severing LONG-TERM supply contracts.

BARTER
Paying for GOODS and SERVICES with other goods and services: that is, transactions that do not involve an exchange of MONEY. Barter can occur at a

basic level (my eggs for your honey) and at a highly sophisticated level (Russian oil for American planes). The more sophisticated version is often referred to as countertrade.

BASE PERIOD
A time in the past used as a yardstick against which to compare future performance of, for example, a BUSINESS or an economy. It is easy to see how an economy has grown, for example, if its GDP is related to a base period in which it was assumed to be 100 units. See also INDEX.

BASE RATE
A declared RATE OF INTEREST that is used in the UK as a reference point for other rates. Thus a BANK might say that its lending rate to a customer is base rate plus three (percentage points).

BASIS POINT
The smallest unit in a measure of INTEREST rates. Thus one basis point in 9.7% is 0.1; one basis point in 9.76% is 0.01.

BEAN COUNTER
An unflattering name for an ACCOUNTANT. It implies that accountants spend their time sitting around counting beans – beans once having been used as a primitive form of MONEY to store and exchange VALUE.

BEAR
An INVESTOR who thinks that the PRICE of a SECURITY is going to fall. A bear sells securities in the expectation of being able to buy them back in future at a lower price. (See also BULL.)

BEARER SECURITY
A BOND or SHARE that gives the rights of ownership (such as VOTING RIGHTS or the right to receive dividends) to whoever holds (or bears) them. This is in contrast to registered securities, which belong to the person or ORGANISATION in whose name they are registered.

BELLWETHER

A SECURITY that is seen as a significant indicator of the direction in which a MARKET's prices are moving. INFORMATION TECHNOLOGY dominates BUSINESS to such an extent these days that many bellwether stocks come from the computer or telecoms industries.

BELOW THE LINE

Items in a PROFIT AND LOSS ACCOUNT that appear below the NET PROFIT figure; that is, items that are taken into account after the figure for net profit has been calculated. Contrast with ABOVE THE LINE.

BENCHMARK

The measure of a BUSINESS FUNCTION or PROCESS that is considered to be best practice for a particular INDUSTRY. The number of cars produced per month by the most efficient up-to-date car FACTORY will be a benchmark for all car manufacturers. So will the lowest percentage of quality defects that any factory achieves.

BENEFIT

An advantage gained by the addition of something extra. For example, customers gain a benefit when companies add extra STAFF to handle their enquiries; products benefit from the addition of new machinery that improves their quality. The addition of these extras bears a COST, however, and needs to be subjected to a COST BENEFIT ANALYSIS. (See also FRINGE BENEFITS.)

BENELUX

The countries of Belgium, the Netherlands and Luxembourg, and the economic union between them. This exists within the rules and structure of the EUROPEAN UNION, all three countries being EU members.

BERNE CONVENTION

An international agreement on the protection of COPYRIGHT. Signatory countries agree to treat artistic works from all member countries equally.

Berne Union
An association of national EXPORT-CREDIT agencies based in Berne, Switzerland. The agencies meet at the Berne Union to discuss issues of common concern.

Bid
The PRICE offered for a SECURITY, a COMPANY or a painting. At the moment that it is offered, a bid is the highest price that any potential BUYER is prepared to pay for what is on offer.

Big-ticket item
CONSUMER GOODS that are of such a high PRICE, such as cars or cookers, that customers often buy them on CREDIT.

Bill
There are at least two BUSINESS meanings:

- A written claim in respect of a DEBT.
- An ADVERTISEMENT of GOODS or SERVICES for SALE, as in bill of fare, or BILLBOARD.

Bill of exchange
See BANK DRAFT.

Bill of lading
The documents giving TITLE to GOODS in transit. They describe the goods, their condition and their destination. They are particularly important as backing for a LETTER OF CREDIT. A clean bill is a bill of lading that is attached by a shipping company to goods that are delivered in perfect condition. Hence the expression "a clean bill of health". If the goods are not as they should be, then the bill contains a clause to that effect, and it is said to be a dirty bill.

Billboard
Boards to which are attached bills; that is, ADVERTISEMENTS. Billboards (also known as hoardings) are usually found close to major transport arteries. In some countries they are strictly controlled by

law; in others less so.

I think that I shall never see
A billboard lovely as a tree
Indeed unless the billboards fall
I'll never see a tree at all.
Ogden Nash

BIS
Short for the Bank for International Settlements, a Basle-based FINANCIAL INSTITUTION that acts as a CENTRAL BANK for central banks. Through it they can CLEAR FUNDS among themselves. The BIS also acts as a talking-shop for bank regulators from around the world.

BIT
See BYTE and DIGITAL.

BLACK LIST
A list of individuals, companies or countries from which certain privileges are withheld. For example, companies that disobey a government-imposed BOYCOTT may find themselves blacklisted and unable to bid for future government contracts.

BLACK ECONOMY
The value of all the BLACK MARKET transactions that take place in an economy. By definition these are immeasurable, but many estimates are made nevertheless. In the United States, the black economy is reckoned to be worth less than 5% of GDP. In Italy some estimates put it as high as 25%; and in many low-income developing countries it is undoubtedly much higher.

BLACK MARKET
A MARKET that operates outside the law and government regulation. Black-market transactions are largely untaxed and unrecorded. They may involve the SALE of smuggled GOODS, stolen goods, or illegally copied goods (watches, for instance).

BLANK CHEQUE
A CHEQUE that is signed by the payer but is left blank as to the payee and/or the amount of money to be paid.

BLISTER PACKAGING
A form of packaging that allows a potential purchaser to see a wrapped-up PRODUCT before purchasing it.

BLOCK TRADING
Trading in big blocks of shares, an activity carried out more often by FINANCIAL INSTITUTIONS than by individuals. It is the WHOLESALE end of the EQUITY MARKET.

BLOCKED ACCOUNT
A BANK ACCOUNT which a court or a government has blocked, thus preventing FUNDS from being withdrawn from it.

BLUE CHIP
A QUOTED COMPANY that has a long record of steadily rising profits and uninterrupted DIVIDEND payments.

BLUE COLLAR
Employees who work in a FACTORY are sometimes referred to as blue-collar workers to distinguish them from their managers (who work in offices and are known as WHITE-COLLAR workers). It was once customary for factory workers to wear blue overalls.

BLUEPRINT
Originally the rough outline of a drawing executed on blue paper and used by printers for guidance. More generally, it is a model of a BUSINESS PLAN or PROCESS.

BOARD
A group of people (called directors) who are appointed by the shareholders of a COMPANY to look after their interests. A board will usually have a

number of executive directors, who are also full-time managers of the BUSINESS; a number of non-executive directors, who may represent particular groups of shareholders; and a SECRETARY, who keeps the MINUTES. (See also ADVISORY BOARD and TWO-TIER BOARD.)

Board meeting
A MEETING of the BOARD. Board meetings usually occur once a month and they follow a prescribed AGENDA and formal rules (which are often laid down by law).

What goes on in the boardroom is a travesty. The chairman doesn't want someone under him who is a threat, so he picks someone a little less capable. It's like an anti-Darwinian theory – the survival of the unfittest.
Carl Icahn, American investor

Bond
An IOU issued by a COMPANY or a government in return for an INTEREST-bearing LONG-TERM LOAN. These IOUS can be bought and sold by investors in a SECONDARY MARKET.

Bonded
When imported GOODS are held (DUTY-free) in a secure depot, called a bonded WAREHOUSE, in their country of destination. The goods are removed from the warehouse as and when they are needed, and only then does any duty on them become due.

Bonus
A payment to shareholders or employees that is over and above what they can contractually expect. In some companies, employees receive an annual bonus that is dependent on the company's performance.

Bonus issue
See SCRIP ISSUE.

Book-keeping
The business of maintaining a financial record of a COMPANY's day-to-day transactions. This record forms the basis of the company's annual ACCOUNTS.

Book value
The VALUE of an ASSET as it is recorded in a COMPANY'S BOOKS. This value may be different from the asset's MARKET value because, for example, accounting convention may dictate that the asset be valued in the books at its purchase PRICE. The purchase price may be well above or well below the asset's current market value.

Books
A COMPANY's basic accounting records in which are recorded the financial details of all transactions undertaken by the company.

Boot
The process of starting up a computer, running the small programs that enable the computer to run larger ones.

Bottom line
The NET PROFIT or LOSS figure in a COMPANY'S ACCOUNTS. More generally, it is the final result of a series of actions or statements. "The bottom line is that the company is BANKRUPT."

Bounce
If a CHEQUE is returned to the payee by the payer's BANK because of a lack of FUNDS it is said to bounce. The payee is asked to represent the cheque in the hope that funds have appeared in the meantime and it can be cleared. If not, it might be returned to the payee yet again, like a rubber ball.

Bourse
French for STOCK EXCHANGE, widely used in the non-English-speaking world.

BOYCOTT
A deliberate decision not to do business with somebody.

BPR
Short for business process RE-ENGINEERING, what happens when BUSINESS processes are radically redesigned to achieve a dramatic improvement in a COMPANY's performance.

BRAINSTORMING
An unstructured MEETING in which the participants attempt to come up with original solutions to corporate problems. The first step is usually an attempt to gather as many ideas as possible. Only later are the ideas evaluated.

BRANCH
The RETAIL OUTLET of a FINANCIAL INSTITUTION. In many countries BANK branches occupy the most prestigious (and expensive) sites on the high streets of towns and cities.

BRAND
The set of values that are signified by a COMPANY's name or symbol and that differentiate it from its competitors. The marketing potential of brands has received much attention in recent years as companies such as Nike, Virgin and Levi have gained great benefit from developing their brands so that they represent more a lifestyle than a product.

BRAND EXTENSION
Extending a BRAND's name to new products or SERVICES. For example, the Swatch car extends the use of the Swatch watch brand to a Mercedes car.

BRAND MANAGEMENT
The process of nurturing and marketing brands so that their VALUE to the BUSINESS increases.

BRANDICIDE
The killing of a BRAND by over-extension. When many different products carry one brand name

there is a danger that the failure of one of the products will reflect badly on all of them. One rotten apple in the barrel can cause the lot to rot.

Breach
The non-performance of something that has been agreed between the parties to a CONTRACT. A breach of contract by one party entitles the other to certain remedies prescribed in law.

Break-even point
The point in the life of a BUSINESS where its REVENUE exceeds its costs. Any new venture's BUSINESS PLAN should contain a clear analysis of when its break-even point will be achieved, and how much it will COST to get there.

Break-up value
The value of a COMPANY when broken up into individual businesses or business units. This may be more or less than the VALUE of the company as a whole. If the value is more and it is a QUOTED COMPANY, it is highly vulnerable to ASSET STRIPPING.

Bretton Woods
A conference held in the US town of Bretton Woods towards the end of the second world war. At the conference a design for the post-war international financial system was drawn up. This included the creation of the WORLD BANK and the IMF.

Bridging loan
A SHORT-TERM LOAN designed to act as a bridge between an item of expenditure and the REVENUE to meet that expenditure. Frequently used in housing finance to fund the purchase of a new home until the borrowers are able to sell their old one.

Broker
An AGENT who buys and sells assets (usually financial assets) on behalf of others, and who is rewarded by a COMMISSION related to the VALUE of the transactions undertaken. A broker can be an individual or a FIRM. (See also STOCKBROKER.)

Brown goods
Electrical CONSUMER GOODS that used to be encased in brown veneer, such as radios and televisions (see also WHITE GOODS).

Brownfield site
A site made available for industrial development which has already been used for commercial purposes. Contrast with GREENFIELD SITE.

Bubble
An artificially inflated financial MARKET. The most famous bubble in history was the South Sea Bubble of 1720 in which the shares of the UK's South Sea Company increased tenfold before collapsing to next to nothing.

Bucket shop
A FIRM of brokers that deals in securities (or airline tickets) of dubious provenance.

Budget
An estimate of future REVENUE and costs over a specific period. Budgets are usually prepared on an annual or a monthly basis. They are drawn up for the finances of large countries and of tiny BUSINESS units alike.

Buffer stock
A STOCK of materials held in reserve. Large COMMODITY markets retain buffer stocks to smooth out the flow of supply and DEMAND. Businesses aim to keep their buffer stocks as low as possible so that they minimise the COST of retaining materials unnecessarily.

Bull
An INVESTOR who expects the PRICE of a SECURITY (or of a securities MARKET) to rise. Bulls buy securities now in the expectation of being able to sell them in the future for a PROFIT. Bulls who are changing their minds are known as stale bulls. Contrast with BEAR.

Bullet loan
A LOAN on which the borrower pays only INTEREST during the life of the loan. The CAPITAL is repaid all at once (in a single bullet) at the end of the term of the loan.

Bullion
Silver or gold that has not been turned into coins. Gold bullion is usually kept in the form of ingots of a standard shape and weight.

Bunching
The practice of accelerating payments (and bringing them closer together) to take advantage of TAX rules.

Bundling
The practice of offering other products or SERVICES that are related to the PRODUCT that is being sold at a special PRICE. SOFTWARE packages, for example, are often bundled with the purchase of HARDWARE.

Bureaucracy
The collection of officials (either within government or within corporate MANAGEMENT) who see that the rules of an ORGANISATION (or of a country) are obeyed. Such officials are the cause of much frustration and the butt of many jokes.

Business
There are three overlapping meanings:

- An ORGANISATION run for PROFIT, be it a COMPANY, PARTNERSHIP or SOLE TRADER;
- The collection of all such organisations;
- The main activity of all of the above.

Business cycle
The economies of most countries move in a cycle of RECESSION followed by recovery, followed by another recession. This cycle is known as the business cycle, and it can vary greatly in duration.

Business ethics
The moral code by which businessmen and women conduct their professional relationships with shareholders, employees, suppliers, customers, and so on. Typical issues in business ethics today are:

- Is it acceptable to pay bribes in countries where this is standard practice?
- To what extent should businesses be held responsible for clearing up industrial sites that they abandon?

Business plan
An outline proposal of a new BUSINESS venture which contains details of costs and revenues and an outline of proposed activity over the next 3–5 years. The plan is designed to persuade potential investors, or those in an organisation with the power of decision over it, that the venture is going to make a handsome RETURN.

Business reply card
A prepaid postcard designed to elicit a response from a CONSUMER. Consumers are often asked to reply to questions on the card relating to a PRODUCT that they have just purchased. The information they provide can then be fed into a customer DATABASE, which a BUSINESS will use to increase its knowledge of its customers and to help it pinpoint those who might buy other products that it sells.

Business schools, out of necessity, are condemned to teach the past.
Mark McCormack

Business school
An educational institution that teaches courses on BUSINESS and often provides customised management development programmes for companies. Most business education used to be done at postgraduate level or on the job. But a growing number of universities now offer undergraduate

business courses.

Business-to-business advertising
ADVERTISING which a BUSINESS aims at other businesses. A SUPPLIER of metal hardness testers, for example, does not want to advertise directly to all consumers but only to companies that need to test metal, such as aircraft manufacturers. Business-to-business advertising generally uses written copy (which can sometimes be highly technical) rather than eye-catching images.

Buy-back
A clause in a purchasing CONTRACT whereby a vendor agrees to buy back GOODS in certain circumstances. For example, a builder might agree to buy back a property at a prearranged PRICE should the purchaser be relocated by his employer within a prescribed period of time.

Buyer
A person or ORGANISATION that has decided to make a purchase.

Buyer's market
A MARKET in which the BUYER has the upper hand, where there is more supply than DEMAND. In such a market COMPETITION should bring prices down. This in turn should eliminate some suppliers (who are no longer able to make a PROFIT) thus restoring the balance between buyers and sellers.

By-product
Something sellable that is produced as an accidental side-effect of manufacturing something else. Sawdust, for example, is a by-product of carpentry, and gas is often a by-product of the oil INDUSTRY.

Byte
A unit for measuring the capacity of a computer. A byte is equal to eight bits (BI…nary digi…TS).

Cabotage
Rights given by law which allow national shippers to carry all cargo (and passengers) transported within the country's territory (by land and sea).

CAD/CAM
Short for computer-aided design and computer-aided manufacturing. These are SOFTWARE programs that assist in design and manufacturing, two business processes that have been dramatically changed by the introduction of computers.

Call
A request made to a COMPANY's investors for payment of what they still owe on shares that the company originally issued as PARTLY PAID.

Call centre
A place where a number of telephone operators are gathered together to take orders on behalf of a COMPANY or to answer customers' queries. Most call centres are part of a large corporation and are used exclusively by its customers and STAFF. But some work as independent organisations and have a number of different clients.

Call option
A contractual right to buy an ASSET (often shares) at a stated price (the STRIKE PRICE) within a specified period of time. If not exercised, a call option expires at the end of the period.

Campaign
Usually used with reference to ADVERTISING. An advertising campaign is a concerted plan to use a number of MEDIA over a given period of time to get a message – such as "this product or company is outstanding" or "don't drink and drive" – from the advertiser across to the general public. A PUBLIC RELATIONS campaign is a planned effort to improve the image of something (a COMPANY, a product or a politician) in the public's eye.

CAP
Short for Common Agricultural Policy, the EUROPEAN UNION's scheme for protecting the incomes of farmers within the EU.

CAP
An upper limit placed on the INTEREST or CAPITAL repayments on a LOAN. Capping can only apply to interest payments whose rates are adjusted according to market conditions. Fixed interest payments are automatically capped.

CAPACITY
The maximum that can be produced by a given unit of LABOUR or CAPITAL in a given period of time.

CAPITAL
The MONEY that is invested in a BUSINESS and that is raised by issuing shares or LONG-TERM bonds. People who invest money in businesses are known as capitalists, and an economic system that allows them to do this is called capitalism. (See also WORKING CAPITAL.)

CAPITAL ALLOWANCE
A part (usually a percentage) of the COST of capital equipment that a COMPANY is allowed to set against its annual INCOME for the purposes of calculating its TAX bill. The rules on capital allowances are to be found in a country's tax legislation.

CAPITAL FLOWS
The movement of capital between countries. Inflows come in, outflows go out.

CAPITAL GAIN
The PROFIT from the SALE of a CAPITAL ASSET (property, art, securities, and so on). In many countries capital gains are subject to special TAX rules.

CAPITAL GOODS
GOODS that are used in the production of other goods: all industrial machinery and OFFICE buildings, as well as road diggers and computers.

CAPITAL INTENSIVE
A BUSINESS, or business PROCESS, that needs a large input of CAPITAL to operate. Capital-intensive businesses include those like steelmaking and vehicle manufacturing which need expensive chunks of PLANT AND EQUIPMENT in order to function.

CAPITALISATION
The attribution of a CAPITAL VALUE to a stream of INCOME; the amount of MONEY that someone is prepared to pay now in order to receive a stream due in the future.

A COMPANY'S market capitalisation is the value that is put on it by a STOCKMARKET, that is the market's value of one SHARE multiplied by the number of shares that have been issued.

CAPITALISE
To turn into CAPITAL. Companies sometimes capitalise expenditure and treat it as a BALANCE SHEET ASSET to be depreciated over a number of years rather than charge it all against the current year's INCOME STATEMENT. For example, many companies capitalise expenditure on R&D.

CAPITAL MARKET
A MARKET in which are traded the financial instruments (such as shares and bonds) which represent the CAPITAL of companies.

CAPTIVE
A service ORGANISATION (usually an INSURANCE BUSINESS) which is owned by a CONGLOMERATE and meets all the conglomerate's needs in its own specialist area. Some captive insurance companies also provide SERVICES for customers outside their own conglomerate.

CAPTIVE MARKET
A MARKET over which a SUPPLIER has special control. For instance, the only newspaper shop in a community of elderly retired people could be said to have a captive market.

CAREER
A way of making a living, used by some to refer only to certain ways of doing so; for example, lawyers have careers; electricians have jobs.

CAREER PATH
The planned direction of a person's CAREER. Choosing a career path determines what TRAINING and future jobs a person should undertake to maintain that direction.

Whom the Gods wish to destroy,
they first call promising.
Cyril Connolly

CARNET
A document authorising its holder to bring SAMPLES through CUSTOMS AND EXCISE without incurring any DUTY (within prescribed limits).

CARRY FORWARD/CARRY BACK
The shifting of payments from one ACCOUNTING PERIOD to another, usually to gain a financial advantage. Carrying a payment forward takes it into a future period; carrying it back takes it into a previous period.

CARTEL
A group of suppliers who get together to control the supply or the PRICE of their PRODUCT. Some cartels, such as OPEC, operate overtly. Others are less easy to pin down. For example, if the prices for electrical GOODS are the same in most shops, is this because the makers have colluded in making retailers charge these prices? Or is it because the MARKET forces retailers not to charge more than their competitors? (See also MONOPOLY.)

CASE STUDY
A formal written description of a BUSINESS problem. Case studies are much used by business schools as a method of teaching MANAGEMENT. Most case studies are of real issues that have been faced by

real companies; a few are fiction.

CASH
Notes, coins and other assets that can be turned rapidly into notes and coins; for example, SHORT-TERM BANK balances or highly liquid securities.

CASH AND CARRY
A half-way house between wholesaling and retailing. An outlet that sells products to the general public at low prices but with a minimum of service. Cash-and-carry outlets frequently demand that customers buy in bulk.

CASH BOOK
A COMPANY'S record of its CASH transactions, both receipts and payments.

CASH COW
A BUSINESS within a group of businesses that generates a lot of CASH which can be used (like the milk of a cow) to nourish other businesses.

CASH DISCOUNT
A DISCOUNT in the PRICE of a PRODUCT granted by a vendor in return for payment in CASH. CREDIT CARD companies often stipulate that outlets which accept their cards may not offer cash discounts to customers.

CASH FLOW
The amount of CASH flowing through an ORGANISATION in a given period. A company's cash flow is equal to its trading PROFIT plus any DEPRECIATION, plus any new MONEY raised through a SHARE ISSUE or a LOAN during the period.

CASH ON DELIVERY
Commonly known by the initials C.O.D. Goods that are shipped on C.O.D. terms to a CUSTOMER must be paid for at the time they are delivered. In the United States the term used is collect on delivery.

CASH REGISTER
A machine which registers the CASH received by vendors from their sales. Often known as the till.

CASTING VOTE
When there is an equal number of votes in favour of and against a proposal, the voting procedures may lay down that somebody has a casting vote to end the deadlock. The CHAIRMAN of a COMPANY'S BOARD of directors, for example, frequently has a casting vote. In effect a person with a casting vote votes twice on issues where the votes are equally divided.

CASUAL LABOUR
Workers who do not have full-time employment and who move from one job to another. In many cases casual labour also moves from one place to another to find paid work. It is often used in agriculture.

CASUALTY INSURANCE
See INSURANCE.

CATALYST
Something which, when added to something else, creates a reaction which neither of the two things could have created on their own. In BUSINESS, MANAGEMENT CONSULTANTS are often said to be catalysts, enabling firms by their mere presence to take action that they would not otherwise have done.

CAVEAT EMPTOR
A Latin expression meaning buyer beware. The best legal advice for consumers in the days before legislation provided them with protection against the SALE of shoddy or defective MERCHANDISE.

CD
See CERTIFICATE OF DEPOSIT.

CENTRAL BANK
An institution that acts as banker to a country's banking system and to its government. Central

banks are also in charge of issuing notes and coins, and they act as a lender of last resort should there be a crisis within the financial system.

CENTRALISATION
The process of concentrating control of a BUSINESS's operations at its centre, usually its headquarters.

CEO
Short for chief executive officer, the person in charge of the day-to-day running of an ORGANISATION. He (or, more rarely, she) is answerable to the BOARD of directors for the organisation's day-to-day performance.

CERTIFICATE OF DEPOSIT
A document issued by a FINANCIAL INSTITUTION as proof of the ownership of a large DEPOSIT of MONEY held with that institution. Certificates of deposit (known as CDS) are negotiable instruments and can be bought and sold in a SECONDARY MARKET.

CERTIFICATE OF INSPECTION
A document certifying that transported goods were in good condition when they began their journey.

CERTIFICATE OF ORIGIN
A document signed by an exporter or by an official body (such as a CHAMBER OF COMMERCE) establishing in which country the GOODS to which the document is attached originated.

CFO
Short for chief financial officer, the person in charge of a COMPANY'S ACCOUNTS and of its finances (raising loans or issuing new securities). The CFO is normally a DIRECTOR of the company and has a seat on the BOARD.

CHAEBOL
A type of CONGLOMERATE peculiar to South Korea. A *chaebol* is similar to a Japanese *keiretsu,* but it is usually family-owned and has less close ties to its suppliers and distributors.

CHAIR
The function of leading a MEETING, and also the OFFICE of the person who carries out that function. For example: "Today Mr Jones will take the chair."

CHAIRMAN
The person who takes the CHAIR at a MEETING. A COMPANY's chairman is the person who takes the chair at the company's BOARD meetings.

CHAMBER OF COMMERCE
A local grouping of businessmen who set out to promote TRADE in their area by acting as a contact point and by providing information.

CHANGE MANAGEMENT
The business of managing changes that are out of the ordinary – a TAKEOVER or the RE-ENGINEERING of a COMPANY, for example.

CHANNEL
See DISTRIBUTION CHANNEL.

CHAPTER 11
A legal status for corporations in the United States that are half-way to BANKRUPTCY. Companies can seek legal protection from their creditors under Chapter 11 of the 1978 Bankruptcy Act. This gives them some time to work out an acceptable solution to their financial difficulties. (See also ADMINISTRATION.)

CHARGE
There are at least two meanings:

- The COST of certain GOODS and SERVICES. BANK CHARGES, for example, are the PRICE paid for receiving banking services.
- A legal document giving rights to property if certain prescribed conditions are met. Banks often take charges on a BUSINESS's assets when they lend it MONEY. The LOAN is then secured and the bank gets its money back – from the SALE of the assets – in the event of

the business failing. (See also FLOATING CHARGE.)

CHARGE CARD
A plastic card issued to consumers which enables them to make cashless purchases at outlets which accept the card. Some charge cards have a CREDIT facility attached which enables cardholders to pay for their purchases over an extended period of time. Charge cards without a credit facility demand that payment be made in full at the end of the month in which the purchases were made. (See also CREDIT CARD.)

CHARTER
A document issued by a recognised authority setting up a corporation and establishing its right to carry on in business. In the UK, for instance, companies established by Royal Charter were set up on the authority of the king or queen of the time.

Charter is also used to refer to the hiring of a vehicle designed to carry a large number of passengers, such as an aircraft or a bus. It originally referred to space rented on a cargo ship.

CHECK
The American spelling for CHEQUE.

CHECKING ACCOUNT
See CURRENT ACCOUNT.

CHEQUE
A method of transferring FUNDS from one party to another via the banking system. Technically, a cheque is a BILL OF EXCHANGE drawn on a BANK and payable on DEMAND. (See also BOUNCE, CROSSED and TRAVELLERS' CHEQUE.)

CHERRY PICKING
The practice of targeting (and obtaining) the best (that is, the most profitable) consumers in a MARKET. Old-established firms in a market resent it greatly when new entrants start cherry picking among their customers.

Chinese wall
A barrier placed between two arms of a BUSINESS so that they work independently of each other to avoid conflicts of interest. Chinese walls are often necessary in financial institutions – for example between the CORPORATE FINANCE and FUND MANAGEMENT sides of an INVESTMENT BANK, to ensure there is no risk of the fund managers benefiting from INSIDE INFORMATION or of helping their corporate finance colleagues out when a new ISSUE of shares is going badly.

Churn
The practice by a BROKER of trading inappropriately on behalf of a CLIENT, purely to generate extra COMMISSION.

CIF
Short for cost, insurance and freight. When added to shipping documents, the letters CIF indicate that the agreed PRICE includes the COST of the GOODS, their INSURANCE in transit and the freight.

Claim
There are two business-related meanings:

- A demand; in particular, one made to an insurer for COMPENSATION for a loss suffered in accordance with the terms of an insurance CONTRACT.
- A right to exploit a piece of land, particularly for its minerals.

Class
A group of people with something in common that enables them to take legal action as a group, in a class action. Shareholders, for instance, from whom vital information about their COMPANY is withheld, could sue as a class.

It is also a group of securities with similar properties, as in Class A shares. (See A AND B SHARES.)

Classified advertisement
A small ADVERTISEMENT, usually in black and white, which is typically no more than one column wide

and paid for on a per-line, per-centimetre or per-word basis. Such advertisements are often called small ads. They are usually grouped together at the back of a newspaper or magazine.

CLAW BACK
A clause in a contract that specifies circumstances in which the seller of goods may be entitled to share in unforeseen profits that are made by the buyer from those goods. Commonly used where state assets are sold off to developers.

CLEAN BILL
See BILL OF LADING.

CLEAR
The process of adding and subtracting a series of amounts owing between organisations so that they can settle their debts with a single payment. Clearing banks clear cheques among themselves at the end of each working day.

GOODS are said to have cleared CUSTOMS when they have passed through customs procedures. They are then free to be traded inside the country into which they have been imported.

CLEARANCE SALE
A special SALE designed to get rid of all of a retailer's stock, or at least all of a particular PRODUCT line.

CLIENT
Professional SERVICES firms, such as lawyers and accountants, have clients; everybody else has customers.

CLOSE COMPANY
A COMPANY whose shares are held by only a few investors. There is thus not a fully open market in the company's shares. Special TAX considerations often apply to close companies.

CLOSED SHOP
A COMPANY where all the workers belong to one

TRADE UNION, and where any job applicant has to be a member of that union before he or she can be employed. In many countries closed shops are illegal.

Closing price
The last PRICE at which a STOCK was traded during a period (usually a day) on a recognised STOCK EXCHANGE.

C.O.D.
See CASH ON DELIVERY.

Code of practice
A list of standards drawn up by an INDUSTRY or professional association that the members of that association agree to be bound by. They do so in the hope of protecting their reputations from rogue practitioners. Those who break the code stand to be disciplined or, in extreme cases, expelled from the association.

Cold calling
The making of unannounced calls on customers (actual or potential). In the past these involved salesman knocking on doors. Nowadays most cold calling is done by telephone, much of it when the recipient has just sat down for a meal.

Collateral
A contractual obligation that exists alongside ("collateral to") another obligation and which provides SECURITY for that obligation. Collateral may take the form of a CHARGE on property as security for a LOAN, or it may be a GUARANTEE. For example, parents often provide collateral for BANK loans to their student offspring.

Collective bargaining
The process of negotiating PAY increases and working conditions between an employer or groups of employers and representatives acting on behalf of a group of employees. Most public-sector pay awards are settled by collective bargaining.

COMFORT LETTER
A letter written by an independent AUDITOR stating that there has been no material change in a COMPANY'S ACCOUNTS between the preparation of a PROSPECTUS for a new SHARE ISSUE and the time that the prospectus is distributed to potential investors. Comfort letters are a requirement of US securities legislation.

COMMERCIAL
There are two definitions:

- Of or to do with commerce; that is, TRADE between different people or organisations.
- An ADVERTISING message that is broadcast on television, on the radio or in the cinema. (See also ADVERTISEMENT.)

COMMERCIAL PAPER
A SHORT-TERM DEBT instrument (usually of 30–90 days MATURITY) issued by a large corporation. Commercial paper does not pay INTEREST. It is sold at a DISCOUNT to its face VALUE and its reward comes from the CAPITAL GAIN on maturity.

COMMISSION
A performance-related payment. Sales STAFF may be paid partly on a commission basis under which they receive a percentage of the amount of sales they make. Agents usually make their money entirely from commission.

COMMITMENT FEE
A payment made to a lender in return for the lender's commitment to make a LOAN available, up to a certain amount and for a prescribed period of time.

COMMITTEE
A group of people who meet on regular occasions to discuss a specified topic. A COMPANY'S BOARD often creates a number of subcommittees to which it delegates responsibility for different functions; for example, directors' REMUNERATION, the

appointment of auditors, and so on. (See also AUDIT COMMITTEE.)

COMMODITY
A PRODUCT which is sold in bulk and is virtually indistinguishable between one producer and another. Some RAW MATERIAL commodities (such as metals and grains) are sold on the floor of an exchange – like securities.

COMMON STOCK
The US term for ORDINARY SHARES.

COMPANY
A legal entity formed by a group of individuals for the purpose of doing BUSINESS. A company has a legal existence that is separate from the individuals who found it. (See also LIMITED LIABILITY, PRIVATE COMPANY and PUBLIC COMPANY.)

COMPANY SECRETARY
Called the corporate secretary in the United States, this is the person charged with seeing that a COMPANY fulfils its legal obligations: that it registers in the proper way; holds formal BOARD meetings as and when it should; and keeps its shareholders properly informed.

COMPARATIVE ADVANTAGE
An economic theory first put forward by David Ricardo in the early 19th century. The theory says that all countries will be better off if each of them concentrates on doing the things it does best, even if what it does second best is better than what another country does best.

COMPENSATING BALANCE
A DEPOSIT placed with a BANK by a borrower in return for a LOAN from the bank.

COMPENSATION
There are two business-related meanings:

- The total package of rewards received by an

EMPLOYEE, including SALARY, PENSION and non-monetary perks such as holiday entitlement.
- The award by a court or tribunal for DAMAGES caused to a plaintiff.

COMPETENCY
The collection of skills, knowledge and personal qualities required to carry out a job. For example, CALL CENTRE operators need to have adequate computer skills and be good with people. (See also CORE COMPETENCE.)

Competition brings out the best in products and the worst in people.
David Sarnoff, founder of RCA

COMPETITION
The battle between individual firms to provide the best VALUE for MONEY to their customers. Competition encourages the most efficient firms to flourish. To maximise economic efficiency, national regulators attempt to create conditions in which competition is as fair as possible. Hence the ANTI-TRUST type of laws that exist in many countries across the world.

I don't meet competition; I crush it.
Charles Revson, founder of Revlon

COMPETITIVE ADVANTAGE
Something which gives one FIRM an edge in competing with others. Such an advantage could be the quality of its INTELLECTUAL PROPERTY or its ability to source high-quality, low-price RAW MATERIALS or LABOUR.

The ability to learn faster than your competitors may be the only sustainable competitive advantage.
Arie de Geus, head of planning at Royal Dutch Shell

Competitor
Any business that is chasing the same customers in the same market as you.

Component
An integral part of another product that is required for its manufacture, such as a microchip in a computer or a headlamp in an automobile.

Compound interest
The interest that is earned during a period when calculated as a percentage of the capital sum plus any interest that has been earned in previous periods. Compound interest assumes that previous interest payments are added to the capital sum and thus increase it.

Compromise
A trade-off of points of equal value in an attempt to reach agreement with another party. The essence of any process of negotiation is a willingness to compromise.

Compulsory retirement
The enforced retirement of an employee because of company rules or national legislation; for example, that directors or judges retire at 70.

Concentration
The extent to which a market is supplied by a small number of organisations. For example, the market for jet aircraft is highly concentrated while the market for chocolate bars is not.

Concert party
A small number of investors who act together in an attempt to control a company in which they hold shares. This is usually achieved by the investors between them obtaining over 50% of the voting rights in the company.

Concession
A special right given to someone in return (usually) for a monetary consideration. For example,

the right to mine a certain piece of land or to sell GOODS on a particular area of floorspace within a DEPARTMENT STORE.

CONCILIATION
The process of attempting to bring together negotiating parties who have ceased to talk to each other, such as MANAGEMENT and a TRADE UNION.

CONFERENCE
There are two business-related meanings:

- A formal gathering of people for the purpose of discussing a particular business issue.
- An agreement between a group of international shippers about the routes that they will sail and the rates that they will charge; an OLIGOPOLY.

CONFERENCE CALL
A telephone call involving more than two people in more than two places. Conference calls enable managers in different offices of the same corporation to have extended discussions without having to travel long distances. Conference calls need to be carefully scheduled in much the same way as face-to-face meetings. (See also VIDEOCONFERENCE.)

CONFLICT OF INTEREST
A clash between the best interests of a person or FIRM in one guise and their best interests in another; for example, as suppliers of SERVICES to two different clients who are competitors. (See also CHINESE WALL.)

CONGLOMERATE
A large GROUP of businesses that are held together in a single corporate STRUCTURE by cross-shareholdings. The businesses within a conglomerate cover a wide range of unrelated industries.

CONSENSUS
In general, any agreement. More specifically, the

agreement among the member countries of the OECD about how far they will subsidise the INTEREST rates on loans to buyers of their countries' EXPORTS.

CONSIGNEE
The individual or COMPANY named in shipping documents as being the ultimate recipient of the GOODS that are being shipped.

CONSIGNMENT
The supply of GOODS to a vendor on the understanding that the vendor will pay for whatever goods he or she is able to sell, and will return the rest to the SUPPLIER.

CONSIGNOR
The individual or COMPANY named in shipping documents as being the original shipper of the GOODS.

CONSOLIDATE
To bring together into a single set of ACCOUNTS the separate sets of all the companies within a single GROUP. In effect, this nets out from the accounts those transactions that have been made between companies within the group.

Also, a number of shipments of FREIGHT can be consolidated into one in order to save costs – the larger the shipment, the lower (in theory) is the cost of freight. Moreover, small shipments are often subject to minimum charges.

CONSORTIUM
A GROUP of companies that come together in some shape for a specific purpose. Most commonly, the members of a consortium take shares in a new entity that is formed expressly for the purpose.

CONSTRUCTIVE DISMISSAL
When there are sufficient grounds for an EMPLOYEE to leave his or her employment, even though he or she has not actually been formally dismissed from that employment. Someone who has been

constructively dismissed may be entitled to COMPENSATION for UNFAIR DISMISSAL.

CONSULTANT
An individual (or a FIRM) that provides professional advice to an ORGANISATION for a FEE. (See also MANAGEMENT CONSULTANT.)

CONSULTING
The BUSINESS of a CONSULTANT.

CONSUMER
Any individual that manufacturers target as a MARKET for their output.

The consumer is not a moron; she is your wife.
David Ogilvy, founder of advertising agency Ogilvy & Mather

CONSUMER CREDIT
Loans given to consumers to enable them to buy the output of producers.

CONSUMER DURABLE
A large PRODUCT sold to the general public and designed to last for a length of time, such as a washing machine.

CONSUMER GOODS
Products which consumers buy regularly to satisfy basic household demands. Contrast with LUXURY GOODS. (See also FMCG.)

CONSUMER PRICE INDEX
An index that measures increases in the prices of GOODS and SERVICES that are sold to the general public. (See also INFLATION.)

CONTAINER
A standardised unit in which GOODS are transported by road, rail or sea.

CONTINGENCY
A financial or commercial possibility. Thus contin-

gency planning is the forming of a plan to seize a commercial opportunity or deal with setbacks in the future.

A contingency FEE is a fee that is paid to a lawyer only if the outcome of the case is favourable; it is usually a percentage of the DAMAGES or compensation awarded in the case.

CONTINGENT LIABILITY
Something that might become a LIABILITY if something else happens. If a COMPANY is involved in a lawsuit for DAMAGES, for instance, there is a liability contingent on the company losing the case.

CONTINUOUS EMPLOYMENT
The guarantee of full-time, non-stop work (within certain prescribed hours) that was the essence of the traditional employment CONTRACT. Employers increasingly prefer to OUTSOURCE work to people when there is work to be done.

CONTINUOUS IMPROVEMENT
A translation of the Japanese word *kaizen*, the MANAGEMENT idea that by making small improvements to all processes all the time, a COMPANY can quite quickly make a dramatic change in its competitiveness.

CONTRACT
A legally binding agreement between two or more people in which each promises to do (or not to do) something. Nobody can be bound by a contract to do something which is itself illegal. Contracts in BUSINESS are usually made in writing, although verbal contracts can be just as binding. The terms of a contract can be express or implied. Express terms have been explicitly stated. Implied terms are those that it is reasonable to imply that the parties agreed to even though they did not "express" them.

CONTRIBUTION
The amount by which a BUSINESS'S REVENUE exceeds its variable costs. This amount is a contribution to

the business's fixed costs. Only if the contribution exceeds the fixed costs will the business make a PROFIT. The contribution after variable costs is sometimes referred to as the gross contribution, with the term net contribution being used to refer to the contribution after both variable and fixed costs; that is, the profit.

CONTROL

An INVESTOR is said to control a COMPANY when the investor owns 51% or more of the company's SHARE CAPITAL.

In MARKETING, a control is a standard response to a marketing effort against which other efforts can be measured. (See also QUALITY CONTROL and STOCK CONTROL.)

CONTROL SYSTEM

A method of ensuring that production or MANAGEMENT processes are carried out correctly. Control systems may be embedded into computer programs, or they may be mechanical systems that are built into production lines to ensure that the right parts arrive at the right time.

CONVENIENCE STORE

A RETAIL OUTLET whose unique appeal is its convenience for customers. To be successful it needs to:

- be open for long hours;
- be located near to its regular customers; and
- sell products that those customers particularly need.

If it achieves these three goals a convenience store can charge PREMIUM prices for its products.

CONVERTIBLE

A SECURITY that can be changed from one form to another when certain circumstances occur. For instance, a BOND that can be converted into EQUITY after a certain date, or an ORDINARY SHARE that can be converted into a PREFERENCE SHARE.

Conveyance
A transfer of the TITLE to property from one person to another.

COO
Short for chief operating officer, the person who has hands-on responsibility for the day-to-day operation of a BUSINESS.

Cooling-off period
A period of time that is required to pass between the signing and the full coming into force of a CONTRACT. In particular, it applies to the time between the filing of a PROSPECTUS for a new ISSUE of securities in the United States and the offering of those securities to the public. Cooling-off periods are designed to protect consumers from overzealous sales techniques

Co-operative
A type of BUSINESS ORGANISATION that is owned collectively by its members. Members run the business for their own mutual benefit rather than for profit. Co-operatives have been particularly popular in the agricultural INDUSTRY and among savings banks.

Copyright
An INTELLECTUAL PROPERTY right, copyright is the ownership of words or other things that can be written down or portrayed graphically.

Core competence
The set of skills and knowledge that sit at the heart of an ORGANISATION (see also COMPETENCY).

Corner
To control so much of the MARKET for a product that you control the PRICE. For example: "Together, the two companies were able to corner the silver market."

Corporate bond
A DEBT instrument issued by a private corporation.

Corporate finance
The process of raising CAPITAL (EQUITY or LONG-TERM DEBT) on behalf of corporations and governments. Corporate finance has traditionally been a speciality of merchant banks in London and of investment banks in New York.

Corporate governance
See GOVERNANCE.

Corporate identity
The collection of characteristics that uniquely identify an ORGANISATION; for example, the arches in the "M" of McDonald's, the colour of the pumps at a Shell filling station, or the environmentally friendly ethos of the Body Shop.

Corporation
See COMPANY.

Corporation tax
The TAX that is charged on a COMPANY'S PROFIT. Rates of corporation tax vary around the world and MULTINATIONAL companies organise themselves to minimise the amount that they have to pay.

Correction
A sudden reversal in the movement of a MARKET. For example, a STOCKMARKET that has been rising strongly all day might have a correction at the end of the day as investors have second thoughts about the market's optimism.

Correspondent bank
See LETTER OF CREDIT.

It's not cheap goods we seek to possess,
but expensive goods that cost a lot less.
Anon

Cost
The amount of MONEY paid to purchase something. (See also AVERAGE, CURRENT, DIRECT, FIXED,

HISTORIC, INDIRECT, MARGINAL, OPPORTUNITY, REPLACEMENT, TRANSFER, UNIT and VARIABLE COST.)

COST ACCOUNTING
A detailed breakdown of the COST of producing GOODS or SERVICES to help calculate a PRICE at which to sell them. (See also COST-PLUS.)

COST-BENEFIT ANALYSIS
A type of analysis that tries to measure the BENEFIT to be gained from an extra COST. For example, what would be the cost of providing a same-day mail service within a major city centre, and how much would customers pay for it.

COST CENTRE
A BUSINESS unit to which costs can be specifically allocated. A cost centre can be as small as a single machine or as large as a major SUBSIDIARY.

COST EFFECTIVE
Something that produces enough benefit to justify its COST is said to be cost effective.

COST, INSURANCE, FREIGHT
See CIF.

COST OF CAPITAL
The average cost to a COMPANY of servicing its CAPITAL: its EQUITY (through DIVIDEND payments) and its loans (through INTEREST payments).

COST OF LIVING
A factor taken into account when an EMPLOYEE is posted to another country or another region. If the cost of living in that region is higher than it is where the employee was originally employed, then he or she may be paid a cost of living allowance (COLA) to compensate for the different PRICE levels.

COST OVERRUN
The amount by which a project exceeds its BUDGET.

Cost-plus
A method of calculating the PRICE at which something is to be sold based on the COST of manufacturing it. Cost-plus starts with this cost and then adds a percentage for PROFIT and for any other hidden costs. (See also COST ACCOUNTING.)

Countercyclical
Something that occurs contrary to the normal BUSINESS CYCLE. For example, when an economy is depressed the BUSINESS of BANKRUPTCY lawyers booms. Their business is said to be countercyclical.

Counterfeit
To imitate the GOODS or SERVICES produced by another manufacturer so closely that they are mistaken for the goods of the other manufacturer. Luxury goods (like Rolex watches and Louis Vuitton bags) are particularly susceptible to counterfeit. Some say it is mankind's second-oldest profession – and no more likely to be stamped out than the oldest.

Counter offer
An offer made in response to another offer. A counter offer has to be more generous than the original offer for it to stand a chance of being accepted.

Countertrade
See BARTER.

Countervailing duty
A DUTY that is imposed by a country on imported GOODS to counter a SUBSIDY that has been granted to the goods by the exporting country.

Country of origin
The country from which GOODS originate. Where quotas are in operation it is important that goods are marked clearly with their country of origin to keep IMPORTS within their QUOTA.

COUPON
A detachable part of a BEARER BOND. The coupon gives its holder the right to the INTEREST payments that are due on the bond.

COVENANT
A contractual promise to do (or not to do) some sort of BUSINESS or financial activity. Someone working for a FIRM in a sensitive INDUSTRY, such as defence, might covenant not to work for any of the firm's rivals for a certain period of time after their employment has ended.

COVER
There are two business-related meanings:

- Protection against financial LOSS, as provided by INSURANCE or by buying assets that reduce the risk of future loss. (See HEDGE.)
- The number of times that a COMPANY'S DIVIDEND or INTEREST payments are covered by its PROFIT.

CPA
See CRITICAL PATH ANALYSIS.

CPM
Short for cost per mille (that is, cost per thousand), a basis for comparing the costs of ADVERTISING in different MEDIA. The CPM is the COST of reaching an audience of 1,000. It does not take into account how many of the 1,000 are awake when the message is conveyed.

CREATIVE ACCOUNTING
Since many of the things that accountants measure are subject to interpretation, it is possible to put a more (or less) favourable tint on a COMPANY'S ACCOUNTS by being creative with that interpretation.

CREDIT
A sum of MONEY made available for a person's (or a COMPANY'S) use. "His credit is good" means that a person has access to FUNDS which enable him to pay his bills as and when they fall due. "She

bought it on credit" means that the purchaser will have a sum of money available in future that will enable her to pay for the GOODS.

CREDIT CARD
A rectangular plastic card issued to a CONSUMER by a FINANCIAL INSTITUTION. Credit cards empower their holders to buy GOODS or SERVICES on CREDIT from organisations which accept such cards as a method of payment.

CREDIT CONTROL
The process of controlling the total amount of CREDIT granted by either a FIRM or an economy. Governments or central banks can control credit by raising the INTEREST RATE; firms can control credit by calling in overdue debts.

CREDIT LINE
An amount of CREDIT that a BANK agrees, in principle, to grant to a CUSTOMER'S ACCOUNT. The customer is then able to draw FUNDS from the account at any time, and up to that limit. In some cases the bank lays down the purposes for which the money may be used.

CREDIT NOTE
Formal notice that a CUSTOMER'S account with a SUPPLIER has been credited with a specific amount. The credit may have arisen because the customer has returned faulty GOODS, or was supplied less than the amount invoiced for.

CREDIT RATING
The contentious practice of ranking the DEBT instruments of corporations and governments according to an independent ANALYST'S assessment of the DEBTOR'S ability to repay them on time.

CREDIT-RATING AGENCY
An organisation that assesses the ability of borrowers to repay their debts on time, and that ranks their ability along the lines of old-fashioned exam results: A+, B-, and so on.

CREDITOR
An individual or ORGANISATION to whom money is owed. The opposite of DEBTOR.

CRISIS MANAGEMENT
The process of managing a crisis, an event or a series of events that are out of the ordinary.

CROSS-DEFAULT
A condition in a LOAN CONTRACT that says that if the borrower defaults on any of its other loans or securities it may be deemed to have defaulted on this one. The lender is then free to seek repayment of the loan as if it were in DEFAULT.

CROSS-RATE
The EXCHANGE RATE between two currencies calculated via a third rate. For example, if there are 2 dollars to 1 pound and 1,000 lira to 1 dollar, the pound/lira cross-rate is 2,000 lira to the pound.

CROSS-SELLING
The practice of placing products that are linked together in the CONSUMER'S mind next to each other on a retailer's shelves; for example, the bacon next to the eggs, or the ties next to the shirts. Also, the attempt to sell one product to a customer who has already bought something completely different from the same seller – when a bank that gave you a loan attempts to sell you insurance as well.

CROSS-SUBSIDISING
Purposely selling one PRODUCT at a LOSS in the knowledge that it is being subsidised by another; for example, a café selling coffee at a low PRICE to entice customers in to buy its cakes at a high price.

CULTURE
The unique ways of doing things and of thinking about things that differentiate one ORGANISATION from another. These are influenced by the organisation's history (by notorious disasters, for example), by its more powerful managers ("Remember

P.J.?") and by its habits (who gets access to the corporate car park).

The only culture in this company is in the yoghurts in the canteen.
American executive

CUM DIVIDEND
A SHARE that is being sold together with the rights to a DIVIDEND that has been announced by the COMPANY but not yet paid.

CURRENCY
The denomination of the notes and coins in circulation in an economy. The UK currency is the pound sterling; the US currency is the dollar; the new European currency is the euro.

CURRENT ACCOUNT
A BANK ACCOUNT, known in the United States as a checking account, the FUNDS of which are used mainly for the purposes of money transmission. Cheques are drawn on current accounts, and standing orders are debited against them. Current accounts rarely pay significant rates of INTEREST on CREDIT balances. (See also BALANCE OF PAYMENTS.)

CURRENT ASSET
Assets on a COMPANY'S BALANCE SHEET that are likely to be sold or transferred (if they are financial assets) during the next ACCOUNTING PERIOD. Current assets include things like CASH, STOCK and ACCOUNTS RECEIVABLE.

CURRENT COST
The present MARKET VALUE of an ASSET.

CURRENT RATIO
The ratio of a firm's current assets to its current liabilities (that is, its SHORT-TERM loans and TRADE debts). The ratio is used as an indicator of a COMPANY'S ability to pay its debts on time, and thus of its LIQUIDITY. (See also WORKING CAPITAL.)

Customer
A person or ORGANISATION who buys FINISHED GOODS or SERVICES, and at whom, therefore, all industrial activity is directed.

To satisfy the customer is the mission and purpose of every business.
Peter Drucker

Customer care
A systematic attempt by an ORGANISATION to take greater care of its customers, and to teach its employees the value of so doing.

The customer is always right.
Gordon Selfridge, founder of the London department store of the same name

Customised
A PRODUCT or service that is adapted specially to suit an individual CUSTOMER.

Customs and Excise
The authority responsible for preventing GOODS from entering a country illegally, and for collecting the tariffs imposed on those imported legally.

Customs duty
A TAX imposed on imported GOODS.

Customs union
An ALLIANCE of a number of countries that agree to remove CUSTOMS AND EXCISE controls on GOODS and SERVICES that pass among them.

CV
Short for curriculum vitae, a summary of a person's career and educational achievements. CVS are invariably required when looking for a new job.

CYCLICAL

The occurrence of events in accordance with a cycle, in particular, the BUSINESS CYCLE. A cyclical STOCK is one that rises and falls in line with the rhythms of the business cycle.

D&O
Short for directors' and officers' liability INSURANCE, a type of insurance policy taken out to protect the directors and senior executives of corporations against being sued as individuals for negligence on the part of their COMPANY. The cost of such insurance can be high, especially in the litigious United States where such suits can result in multi-million-dollar awards. It is sometimes known as INDEMNITY insurance.

DAMAGES
A legal award of monetary compensation to a person or BUSINESS who has suffered loss or injury caused by another. For example, a business may have suffered a loss as a result of a BREACH of CONTRACT, or an EMPLOYEE may have been injured as a result of using an unsafe piece of equipment at his or her place of work.

DATABASE
A collection of information stored electronically on a computer.

DATA MINING
The use of sophisticated computer programs to search systematically through a large DATABASE. Such programs are particularly useful to MARKETING departments which want to identify a subset of a large population (all the males in Arkansas, for instance, whose birthdays are next Monday).

DATA WAREHOUSING
The process of organising the storage of large quantities of electronic data in such a way that it best meets the needs of the ORGANISATION to whom it belongs.

DATA PROTECTION
The right of individuals to have access to information about themselves that is held by other parties, such as financial institutions, CREDIT-RATING agencies or government offices. Individuals usually have to submit a formal request to gain access to

the information. Such rights are established in many countries by so-called data protection legislation.

DATE STAMP
A mark on perishable GOODS indicating the date by which they should be sold, and also the date by which they should be consumed. In many countries date stamping is required by law.

DAWN RAID
The purchase in the early hours of the morning, as soon as the STOCKMARKET opens, of a substantial chunk of a COMPANY'S shares, frequently to strengthen a subsequent TAKEOVER bid. Hence, any early-morning BUSINESS practice that is designed to catch someone (especially a COMPETITOR) unawares.

DCF
See DISCOUNTED CASH FLOW.

DEADLINE
A time scheduled for the completion of a task, commonly used to describe the time by which journalists must file their stories to their newspapers. If a deadline that has been set in a CONTRACT is not met, legal consequences may follow.

DEALER
A person who deals in GOODS or SERVICES, buying them in his own right to sell them on to someone else. Contrast with a BROKER, who never takes TITLE to the goods he is broking.

Deals aren't usually blown by principals; they're blown by lawyers and accountants trying to prove how valuable they are.
Robert Townsend

DEBENTURE
A DEBT that is secured only on the good name of the borrower. It has no CHARGE on the borrower's assets.

DEBIT CARD
A rectangular plastic card with a black magnetic strip on the back that can be used to purchase GOODS and SERVICES. A debit card is a bit like a CREDIT CARD, but with one crucial difference. A debit card pays for the goods immediately out of a BANK ACCOUNT somewhere. If there is no credit in the account the purchase will not be authorised. A credit card, however, allows payment to be made later and provides the user with a LOAN to make the purchase.

DEBRIEFING
A MANAGEMENT practice in which an EMPLOYEE describes their experience (with, say, a potential overseas CUSTOMER) to others within their ORGANISATION. The idea is that everyone should learn from the experience of each individual. This is at the heart of a LEARNING ORGANISATION.

DEBT
An obligation on a person or ORGANISATION to pay something (usually MONEY) to another person or organisation.

DEBT-EQUITY RATIO
The ratio of a COMPANY'S DEBT to its EQUITY, more commonly known as gearing, or in the United States as leverage. If the ratio is high, banks are reluctant to lend the company more MONEY.

DEBT SERVICE
The ability of an ORGANISATION (be it a COMPANY or a country) to service its debts – that is, to pay INTEREST and CAPITAL as and when due – out of its CASH FLOW.

DEBTOR
A person or ORGANISATION that owes somebody something.

DECENTRALISATION
The process of moving corporate functions (and the decision-making powers that go with them)

away from a COMPANY's head OFFICE. Many companies are highly decentralised in some respects (say, MARKETING) and highly centralised in others (ACCOUNTS or HUMAN RESOURCES).

DECISION TREE
A diagram that illustrates the consequences of making different decisions, and of the decisions that flow from those consequences.

The man who is denied the opportunity to take important decisions begins to regard as important the decisions that he is allowed to take.
C. Northcote Parkinson

DECLINING BALANCE
A method of DEPRECIATION that depreciates an ASSET by a fixed percentage of its outstanding VALUE at the end of each year, instead of by a fixed percentage of its original value. (See STRAIGHT-LINE DEPRECIATION.)

DEDUCTIBLE
An EXPENSE that can be deducted from a COMPANY's REVENUE for the purposes of calculating its TAX LIABILITY.

DEEP DISCOUNT
A large DISCOUNT on the PRICE of GOODS or SERVICES, probably more than 25%.

DEFAULT
The failure of a borrower to repay a LOAN or SECURITY according to the terms and conditions of the CONTRACT. Once a borrower is in default there are a number of legal options open to lenders for retrieving their MONEY.

Default is also the software PROGRAM that a computer follows if it is not instructed to the contrary.

DEFECTIVE
Not legally binding, as in defective TITLE to a property. A defective title may have been obtained

fraudulently, or there may have been an error in drawing up the CONTRACT.

Defective GOODS are those that do not meet the standard that a CONSUMER might reasonably expect. In most countries a consumer is legally entitled to exchange defective goods or obtain a refund.

DEFERRED

The postponement of a payment (or RECEIPT) from one ACCOUNTING PERIOD into another; for example, deferred TAX.

DEFERRED SHARE

A SHARE in a COMPANY that receives no payment in the event of a LIQUIDATION until all preference and ordinary shareholders have been paid the NOMINAL VALUE of their shares in full. Deferred shares are usually held by people who have a special relationship with the company, such as its founders.

DEFICIT

An excess of spending over REVENUE. This may be by a government (as in the federal BUDGET deficit), by a country (as in a TRADE deficit), or by a COMPANY (which then needs to fund its deficit).

DEFLATION

An across-the-board decrease in prices. Falling prices are dangerous for BUSINESS since they can result in a COMPANY having to sell its output for less than its COST. (See also INFLATION.)

DELAYERING

The removal of layers of MANAGEMENT from the middle levels of an ORGANISATION, thus flattening the organisation and shortening the lines of communication within it.

DELEGATION

The transfer of authority from one person to another (who is generally lower down the corporate hierarchy). Delegation involves the transfer of authority but not of responsibility. EMPOWERMENT attempts to transfer both.

Delinquency
In business, the failure to make payments as and when they fall due.

Delisting
The removal of a quoted SHARE from a STOCK EXCHANGE's list, usually for failing to follow the rules of the exchange. A COMPANY's shares may also be delisted if the company has been taken over by another and has ceased to have an independent existence.

Delivery
The transfer of the TITLE to an ASSET from one owner to another. Thus a delivery note is the document authorising the transfer; the delivery date is the date on which the transfer formally takes place.

Demand
A fundamental concept in ECONOMICS (see also SUPPLY). The extent to which consumers are prepared to pay for GOODS and SERVICES. It is also the right to instantaneous gratification, as in payable on demand or demand DEPOSIT – MONEY in an ACCOUNT that can be withdrawn on demand.

Demerger
The unravelling of a MERGER, or the separation of companies (or of BUSINESS units) that are being run under one corporate umbrella.

Demographics
The study of populations according to social characteristics such as their age, income, family size, and so on. Demographics is particularly helpful to advertisers and MARKETING departments.

Denomination
The number of units of a single note or coin; for example, 1 D-mark, 10 francs, 100 dollars.

Department store
A large RETAIL OUTLET that stocks a wide range of GOODS, from kitchen utensils to make-up. Tradition-

ally located in the centre of big cities, department stores have been hit by the growth of out-of-town shopping malls and of city-centre rents.

Deposit
There are several meanings including:

- MONEY left as SECURITY before the receipt of a service, as when renting an apartment.
- Money left with a BANK for safe-keeping.
- RAW MATERIALS found underground, such as mineral deposits.

Deposit account
An ACCOUNT at a BANK in which a CUSTOMER leaves MONEY for some period of time and on which he earns INTEREST.

Deposit protection
A form of INSURANCE which covers depositors against the loss of their MONEY should their BANK go bust. Deposit protection schemes are usually backed by the state, and they usually cover only a percentage of the total deposits.

Depreciation
The loss of an ASSET'S VALUE as a result of wear and tear and the passage of time. Companies are allowed to set off this amount against their taxable profits – in theory enabling them to put aside untaxed FUNDS with which to replace the depreciating asset at the end of its useful life. (See also DECLINING BALANCE and STRAIGHT LINE.)

Depression
A prolonged and steep decline in a country's GDP, a period when much industrial activity ceases.

Deregulation
The removal of government regulations and of red tape that restrict the ability of firms within an INDUSTRY to compete freely. Industries such as telecoms, banking and aviation have been considerably deregulated in recent years.

Derivative
A financial ASSET that is derived from another financial asset. Thus an OPTION to buy a SHARE is a derivative. The option could not exist without the share, from which it is derived. Some derivatives are extremely complex creations.

Derived demand
DEMAND for things that occurs because of the demand for other things. Thus the demand for CAPITAL GOODS can be said to be derived from the demand for CONSUMER goods. Once consumers start spending, producers begin to invest in PLANT AND EQUIPMENT.

Desktop publishing
Using a collection of computers, SOFTWARE and printers that can fit on a desk in order to produce publications of a quality that used to be possible only in printing plants.

Devaluation
A lowering of the VALUE of a country's CURRENCY vis-à-vis other countries' currencies. This can be done either by MARKET forces or by government forces.

Developer
Someone who adds VALUE to land by building on it or by otherwise turning it into an ASSET that can produce a stream of INCOME.

Development
See R&D.

Differentiation
The process of establishing the way in which a COMPANY's products or SERVICES differ from those of its rivals (how Pepsi tastes different from Coke, for example), and then reinforcing that difference in the CONSUMER's mind by ADVERTISING and PROMOTION.

DIGITAL
The representation of data by a series of digits. In a digital computer, information is transmitted as a row of binary digits, 0 or 1, represented by "on" or "off". In an analogue (or analog) computer, information is represented by some variable physical property (such as an electric voltage).

DILUTE
To reduce the VALUE of existing shares in a COMPANY by issuing new shares at a PRICE lower than the shares' current MARKET value.

DIMINISHING RETURNS
The phenomenon whereby the addition of extra resources to a production PROCESS fails to produce the same additional VALUE. The law of diminishing returns is said to have set in. (see LAW OF DIMINISHING RETURNS.)

DIRECT COST
A COST that can be directly attributed to a particular production PROCESS. Direct costs rise in proportion to the number of units produced. (See also INDIRECT COST and OVERHEAD.)

DIRECT DEBIT
An instruction from a CUSTOMER to a BANK requesting the bank to debit the customer's ACCOUNT with whatever sums are demanded by a named CREDITOR. Direct debits make life easier (and therefore cheaper) for organisations like telephone and electric utilities which receive payments that are regular in time but irregular in amount.

DIRECT MAIL
The SALE and PROMOTION of GOODS and SERVICES by mail. Direct mail is a fast-growing DISTRIBUTION CHANNEL in many countries, despite a widespread belief that most direct mail is thrown away unread.

DIRECT MARKETING
The selling of products and SERVICES directly to the

final CONSUMER by the original producer. Direct MARKETING cuts out intermediaries (such as shops) in the SUPPLY CHAIN. But it often involves substantial costs in reaching the consumer in other ways; for example, by DIRECT MAIL.

DIRECT TAXATION
Taxation that is imposed directly on an individual (for example, INCOME TAX) or a COMPANY (CORPORATION TAX). Contrast with INDIRECT TAXATION.

DIRECTOR
Strictly speaking, a member of the BOARD of a COMPANY who has been properly appointed by the company's shareholders to look after their interests. In many companies, however, people have titles containing the word director even though they are not on the board. In this context, a director is no more than a senior manager.

DIRTY BILL
See BILL OF LADING.

DIRTY FLOAT
A government policy of generally allowing its CURRENCY'S EXCHANGE RATE to float freely according to MARKET DEMAND, but on occasions deciding to intervene in order to adjust the rate to suit other priorities. This is also known as a managed float.

DISCHARGE
The FULFILMENT of (and release from) an obligation. In many countries the restrictions on people declared bankrupt apply only for a certain length of time. At the end of that time, the bankrupt is said to be discharged.

DISCLOSURE
The legal requirement of companies to reveal information to certain parties at certain times. Hence, for example, a DIRECTOR must disclose to fellow directors if he has a financial interest in a COMPANY to which the BOARD is about to award a CONTRACT.

DISCOUNT
The verb to discount means to sell at a reduced PRICE; the noun discount is the amount by which the PRICE is reduced. (See also CASH DISCOUNT and TRADE DISCOUNT.)

DISCOUNT RATE
In general, the rate of INTEREST that is represented by the DISCOUNT to its VALUE on MATURITY at which a financial instrument is sold. Thus if a $100 BOND is due to be repaid in a year's time, and somebody is prepared to pay $95 for it today, the discount rate is the $5 discount at which the bond is being sold, divided by the $95 that is being paid for it (that is, 5.26%).

DISCOUNT STORE
A store selling a wide variety of GOODS, many of them at a DISCOUNT to their normal RETAIL PRICE.

DISCOUNTED CASH FLOW
Popularly known as DCF, a method of calculating the present VALUE of a future stream of INCOME and/or CAPITAL. It discounts the future value of expected flows of CASH in order to find their NET PRESENT VALUE.

DISCRIMINATION
Treating someone differently because of a particular attribute that they have, such as their sex, their religion, or their colour. In many countries discrimination in the workplace is illegal.

DISINFLATION
A slowing down in the rate of INFLATION. Not to be confused with DEFLATION.

DISINTERMEDIATION
The process by which financial intermediaries are cut out of the business of allocating savings. This happens in a number of ways; for example, when companies raise EQUITY directly from the public, or when governments promote savings schemes that attract MONEY directly from consumers.

Disk
The part of a computer where information is stored and which acts as its memory. Floppy disks are light and detachable (but far from floppy) rectangular pieces of plastic and metal on which can be stored electronic data. They enable information to be transferred easily from one stand-alone computer to another. Optical disks and compact disks are disks that hold considerably more data than floppy disks. The non-detachable part of a computer's memory is called the hard disk.

Dismissal
The ending of an individual's CONTRACT of employment with an ORGANISATION. Depending on the nature of the dismissal (for example, by REDUNDANCY) the individual may be entitled to a lump sum on the termination of the contract. If individuals think that they have been unfairly dismissed they may have the right to sue their EMPLOYER. (See UNFAIR DISMISSAL.)

Distress sale
A sale that occurs when owners of goods find themselves in a position of having to sell those goods at a DEEP DISCOUNT – often because of CASH FLOW difficulties.

Distribution
There are two meanings:

- The process of getting FINISHED GOODS into the hands of consumers.
- The way in which something is shared out; a PRODUCT in a particular MARKET, for example, or wealth in a country.

Distribution channel
A route by which GOODS are distributed by a manufacturer to a final CONSUMER.

Diversification
The spreading of a COMPANY'S RISK by its participation in a number of different businesses. A move

by an INSURANCE company into retailing is one example of diversification. It is a way of ensuring that not all the company's eggs are in one industrial basket.

DIVESTMENT
The selling off by a COMPANY of businesses that do not fit in with its general STRATEGY.

DIVIDEND
The part of a COMPANY'S EARNINGS that is distributed to its shareholders in return for their CAPITAL. Dividends are paid regularly (usually half-yearly) and are related to the surplus that the company makes over and above the essential costs of its BUSINESS. The size of a dividend payment, therefore, is some indication of a company's success.

DIVIDEND COVER
The number of times that a COMPANY'S annual DIVIDEND is covered by its annual EARNINGS, that is, its PROFIT divided by its dividend.

DIVISION
An independent unit within a COMPANY.

DIVISION OF LABOUR
The breaking up of a production PROCESS and its DISTRIBUTION among a number of workers so that it is carried out in the most efficient way.

DOCUMENTARY CREDIT
A method of financing TRADE in which the documents proving that a SALE has been made are used as COLLATERAL for a LOAN.

DOMICILE
The home of an individual or a COMPANY for TAX purposes. Each person or company can have only one domicile (so it is not the same as RESIDENCE or nationality). A company's domicile is usually the place of its head OFFICE, an individual's is usually their main place of residence.

Door-to-door
A once-popular but now little used method of selling in which a SALESMAN goes from one house to the next, attempting to persuade the occupier to purchase GOODS or SERVICES. Traditionally used for selling INSURANCE and encyclopaedias.

Dormant company
A COMPANY that is not currently trading. It has a registered name, directors, ARTICLES OF ASSOCIATION, and so on. But it has no TURNOVER.

Double-entry book-keeping
A fundamental principle of accounting whereby every entry into a COMPANY'S BALANCE SHEET has an equal and opposite counterpart: every ASSET has a balancing LIABILITY. A new FACTORY is recorded as an ASSET; the money used to buy it is recorded as a liability.

Double-taxation agreement
An agreement between two countries designed to ensure that companies and individuals are not taxed on the same bit of INCOME in both jurisdictions. The agreements lay out rules as to who has the right to tax which bit of PROFIT, DIVIDEND, INCOME or whatever.

Double time
Any period of time during which an EMPLOYEE is paid double the normal rate – for example, for working on a Sunday or a public holiday.

Dow Jones
The best-known INDEX of movements in the PRICE of US stocks and shares. The main index, the Dow Jones Industrial Average, was founded in October 1896 and measures the price movements of leading shares quoted on the New York Stock Exchange.

Download
To transmit electronically stored information from one computer to another, or from a hard DISK to a floppy disk.

DOWNMARKET
A MARKETING term based on a theoretical division of markets into a top, a middle and a bottom. A PRODUCT aimed to appeal to the bottom end of the market is said to be downmarket. The division of markets can be based on social class, wealth or lifestyle. Contrast with UPMARKET.

DOWNSIZING
A corporate STRATEGY aimed at producing the same amount of output from a smaller quantity of resources (of land, LABOUR or CAPITAL). The RESOURCE that gets hit first in downsizing is usually labour. In the early 1990s downsizing became almost synonymous with REDUNDANCY.

Downsizing and restructuring only mean doing less with less. Re-engineering, by contrast, means doing more with less.

Michael Hammer and James Champy

DOWNSTREAM
An expression used (particularly in the oil INDUSTRY) to indicate an activity that is close to the final CONSUMER. A filling station is much more downstream than an oil rig, for example.

DOWNTIME
The amount of time that is lost during a production PROCESS in maintaining the machinery or in waiting for essential inputs. In most companies the amount of downtime has been falling sharply in recent years.

DUAL PRICING
Asking different prices for the same GOODS and SERVICES in different markets. Dual pricing may give rise to accusations of DUMPING.

DUE DATE
The date on which an obligation is due to be met; for example, the payment of INTEREST or PRINCIPAL on a LOAN.

Due diligence
A thorough search of a COMPANY's businesses carried out by the manager of a new ISSUE of the company's securities or by representatives of another company that is interested in taking it over. If the searchers find that things are not as they had been led to believe, they have grounds for withdrawing from the deal.

Dumping
When the PRICE at which a COMPANY sells its output on a foreign MARKET is less than the price at which it sells it on its home market, the company is said to be dumping its GOODS on to the export market. Under the terms of international free-TRADE agreements, countries are allowed to impose rules that penalise the practice of dumping. However, such anti-dumping rules are extremely hard to enforce.

Durable goods
Products which consumers buy only rarely. These are more durable than the foodstuffs and garments that they purchase at regular (short) intervals. Cars, televisions and washing machines are all examples of durable goods.

Dutch auction
An AUCTION in which the prices called out by the auctioneer start at a high level and then fall lower and lower. The successful bidder is the person who makes the first BID, and not (as in more traditional auctions) the person who makes the last bid.

Duty
A TAX imposed on GOODS or SERVICES as they are traded (for example, import duties) or as they are consumed (for example, the duty on tobacco or alcohol).

Earnings
A commonly used expression in America for a COMPANY'S NET PROFIT. (See also RETAINED EARNINGS.)

Earnings per share
The NET PROFIT (or EARNINGS) of a COMPANY divided by the number of ordinary shares in issue. Earnings per share (EPS) is a useful way to measure a company's performance over time, and its performance relative to other companies.

Earnout
A method of buying a COMPANY which relates the PRICE to its future earnings. This is popular when the company is being sold by its present managers to an outsider who is keen to ensure not only that the managers stay on, but also that they are motivated to maximise the company's earnings in the future.

EBRD
Short for the European Bank for Reconstruction and Development, a London-based international FINANCIAL INSTITUTION set up to help channel FUNDS from the West to Russia and other countries of eastern Europe as they emerged from decades of communism.

E-commerce
Short for electronic commerce, the transacting of BUSINESS electronically, largely via the INTERNET.

Economic life
The length of time during which a machine or a piece of equipment will produce more REVENUE than it costs to maintain it.

Economics
How the world makes a living or, more specifically, how resources (land, LABOUR and CAPITAL) are used to produce GOODS and SERVICES to meet human wants. When one early economist, Thomas Malthus, believed that resources were so scarce that the world was permanently on the

edge of famine, economics came to be known as the dismal science.

Economies of scale
Factors which cause the AVERAGE COST of producing something to drop as output is increased, or the savings that can be made by manufacturing GOODS or supplying SERVICES in large quantities. This is the principle behind all MASS PRODUCTION. Whereas a COMPANY'S DIRECT COSTS increase in direct proportion to the volume of its output, its overheads do not. Whatever number of widgets a company produces, it needs only one HEADQUARTERS, one BOARD, and one CEO.

Economies of scope
The savings that can be made by producing a broad range of GOODS or SERVICES. A BANK, for instance, may find that it costs only a little bit more for it to sell INSURANCE products at the same time and the same place as it sells loans.

Efficiency
The relationship between the input into a machine and the output from the machine. The term is extended to refer to human machines: some workers are more efficient than others.

The world has more bright people than effective people.
Dick Brown, CEO of Cable & Wireless

EGM
Short for extraordinary general meeting, a special MEETING of a COMPANY's shareholders called to consider matters that cannot wait until the company's next annual general meeting (AGM).

Elasticity
The amount by which one thing changes for each unit change in something else. The elasticity of SUPPLY and DEMAND are the amounts by which the production or consumption of GOODS or SERVICES

change for each unit change in PRICE.

E-MAIL
Short for electronic mail, the production and distribution of messages electronically; literally, a form of paperless post. There are semi-public ways of sending e-mail (via the INTERNET) and there are private networks for sending e-mails, between employees of the same FIRM, for example. Such a private NETWORK is referred to as an INTRANET.

EMBARGO
A ban on transferring something from one party to another. It may be GOODS, such as a TRADE embargo preventing the export of arms to a particular country. Or it may be information, for example: "This news is embargoed until midday tomorrow".

EMERGING ECONOMY
A country that is on the way to becoming a developed economy in terms of its GDP per head, and its financial and industrial structure.

EMI
Short for European Monetary Institute, the Frankfurt-based CENTRAL BANK established as part of EMU.

EMPLOYEE
Someone who works for an ORGANISATION doing a defined job for an agreed amount of COMPENSATION.

EMPLOYER
Someone who employs others to perform stipulated tasks in return for monetary rewards.

EMPLOYMENT AGENCY
An agency that tries to match the needs of employers with those of employees. Many agencies specialise in finding workers with particular sorts of skill, such as computer, secretarial or accounting.

EMPOWERMENT
The concept of giving employees the freedom to take as many decisions for themselves as possible.

EMU
Short for Economic and Monetary Union, a series of steps whereby the members of the EUROPEAN UNION bring their monetary and EXCHANGE-RATE policies into line. (See also EURO.)

ENDORSEMENT
A signature on the back of a CHEQUE or other financial instrument by the payee. It effectively transfers the ownership of the instrument from the signatory to the bearer. In advertising, an endorsement is the recommendation of a product by a well-known person.

END USER
The ultimate user of a product who is not necessarily the purchaser of it; for example the driver of a company car.

ENTREPRENEUR
A person who recognises a MARKET opportunity, raises the resources necessary to exploit it, and personally bears some of the RISK. The term was used by a French economist, Jean-Baptiste Say, to describe someone who "shifts economic resources out of an area of lower and into an area of higher productivity and greater yield".

I think if we want to understand the entrepreneur, we should look at the juvenile delinquent.
Abraham Zaleznik, a professor at Harvard Business School

ENVIRONMENTAL AUDIT
An AUDIT of a COMPANY's impact on the environment. The International Chamber of Commerce's definition is: "A management tool comprising a systematic, documented, periodic and objective evaluation of how well (the company's) environ-

mental ORGANISATION, management and equipment are performing."

EPS
See EARNINGS PER SHARE.

EQUAL OPPORTUNITY
The idea that all men and women should have an equal opportunity to do any particular job. Much progress has been made in ensuring that this is the case, but there are still exceptions, as is apparent from the small number of women in senior positions in big corporations.

EQUITY
The RISK CAPITAL supplied by shareholders to a BUSINESS and the balancing item in a COMPANY'S BALANCE SHEET – the amount by which its assets exceeds its other liabilities (to bankers, suppliers, and so on). This is the company's surplus FUNDS, which belong equitably to its shareholders.

ERGONOMICS
The study of the way in which people work, and of the ways in which this (and the machines that they use) can be improved in order to make them more efficient.

ESCROW
When a CONTRACT or an ASSET such as MONEY is placed with a THIRD PARTY until certain conditions are met, it is said to be held in escrow. Parties that are in dispute over the ownership of an asset may agree to place the asset in escrow until an ARBITRATOR has had time to decide who is the rightful owner.

ESTIMATE
An approximate PRICE given by somebody for something that they wish to sell to a potential CUSTOMER.

ETHICAL INVESTMENT
The idea, promoted particularly by certain funds

in the United States, of investing only in companies that meet specific ethical criteria. Companies that do not do business with fascist regimes, for example, or do not massively pollute the environment.

ETHICS
See BUSINESS ETHICS.

EURO
The name of the EUROPEAN UNION's single currency, introduced gradually from January 1999 into willing countries that meet certain prescribed economic criteria. The euro should replace national currencies in these countries during 2002. Thereafter, no more D-marks, no more francs.

EURODOLLAR
The name given to dollars held outside the United States, particularly those held by European banks and by American banks in Europe.

EUROMARKET
A MARKET in financial instruments that are denominated in a currency other than that of the market in which they are traded; for example, a Zurich-based market in dollar-denominated corporate bonds.

EUROPEAN COMMISSION
The executive organ of the EUROPEAN UNION, run by 20 commissioners (two each from France, Germany, Italy, Spain and the UK, and one from each of the other ten member states). The commission drafts legislation in the form either of regulations or directives. Regulations are passed through the European Parliament and apply in all member states. Directives leave the means of achieving the desired result up to individual member states.

EUROPEAN UNION
The community of powerful European countries set up in 1957 by the Treaty of Rome and fired by the desire of its founders to avoid yet another pan-

European war. The members of the EU are gradually bringing their economic and monetary affairs closer and closer together. The original six members were Belgium, France, Italy, Luxembourg, the Netherlands and West Germany. They were joined by Denmark, Ireland and the UK in 1973, Greece in 1981, Portugal and Spain in 1989, and Austria, Finland and Sweden in 1995. (See also EMU.)

EXCHANGE CONTROL
Government-imposed controls that restrict the amount of CURRENCY (domestic and foreign) that can be brought in or out of a country by individuals and corporations.

EXCHANGE RATE
The amount of MONEY denominated in one CURRENCY that can be obtained for a unit of another. Most countries express their currency first and foremost in terms of the US dollar.

EXCISE
A selective TAX imposed on the consumption of GOODS and SERVICES. (See also CUSTOMS AND EXCISE.)

EX-DIVIDEND
An expression used to refer to a SHARE PRICE that does not incorporate a DIVIDEND payment that has been declared by the COMPANY but not yet paid. The dividend in question goes to a previous owner of the share.

EX-FACTORY
An annotation added to a PRICE to indicate the point at which the PRICE applies, in this case when it leaves the FACTORY. In other words, the cost of delivery is extra. Similarly, a price could be ex-WAREHOUSE or ex-customs.

EX GRATIA
An extra payment made to an EMPLOYEE "out of thanks". A feature of an ex-gratia payment is that the payer is under no contractual obligation to make it.

Ex officio
A Latin expression for something that arises "out of the OFFICE" – belonging to somebody because of the office that they hold rather than because of the person that they are. For example, many of the duties of the CHAIRMAN of a COMPANY (such as making the CASTING VOTE at a BOARD MEETING) arise from the fact that he or she occupies the office of chairman, not because they have been chosen as individuals to carry out that duty.

Ex-rights
A note added to the QUOTATION of a SHARE PRICE to indicate that anybody buying the share at that price does not get the benefits of a declared (but not yet issued) RIGHTS ISSUE.

Ex-works
The same as EX-FACTORY.

Executive
Someone who has the power to decide that tasks should be executed. The word usually refers to managers at senior levels.

Executive director
Strictly speaking, a COMPANY EXECUTIVE who is also a DIRECTOR, that is, who serves on the company BOARD. The term director is, however, sometimes used loosely as a title for someone not on the board. In this case an executive director is just a senior executive. (See also NON-EXECUTIVE DIRECTOR.)

Exercise
Making use of a right given under the terms of a CONTRACT. For instance, the OPTION to purchase a SHARE at a certain PRICE and within a certain time; or the right to take up a RIGHTS ISSUE.

Exit route
The way in which an INVESTOR hopes to realise a CAPITAL GAIN from an INVESTMENT. With investment in a BUSINESS, this usually involves floating the

business on a STOCKMARKET and selling shares to the general public. In a more general sense, an exit route can be any STRATEGY for withdrawing from a particular course of action.

EXPATRIATE
A person living and working in a foreign country. The TAX position of expatriates can become complicated because they fall under at least two jurisdictions. Expatriates often enjoy a lifestyle above what they might expect at home because they get PERKS to compensate for the "hardship" of their posting.

EXPENSE
A COST incurred in the legitimate running of a BUSINESS. Expenses can be deducted from the REVENUE of the business before calculating its PROFIT for TAX purposes.

EXPENSE ACCOUNT
An allowance given to an EXECUTIVE for the purposes of entertaining and/or travelling in pursuit of BUSINESS.

EXPORTS
GOODS or SERVICES that are sold to someone or some organisation outside the country in which they are produced.

EXPORT CREDIT
A LOAN given to an exporter in which the GOODS being exported provide SECURITY for the loan. An export credit is designed to bridge the gap between the time when an exporter receives an ORDER and the time when it receives payment. With large CAPITAL GOODS this can be many months, if not years.

EXPORT CREDIT AGENCY
An ORGANISATION set up to administer EXPORT CREDIT guarantees. Such agencies also sometimes lend MONEY directly to foreign buyers to enable them to buy GOODS from the country of the agency. These

loans are frequently granted at favourable rates of INTEREST, involving an element of SUBSIDY to the overseas buyer.

EXPORT CREDIT GUARANTEE
A scheme set up (usually by a government or government agency) to help its countries' exporters by giving guarantees to bankers that their loans to those exporters will be repaid.

EXPORT INSURANCE
An INSURANCE policy taken out to reduce the RISK of loss of exported GOODS while they are in transit.

EXPOSURE
The extent to which a CREDITOR is vulnerable to a particular DEBTOR. For example, a BANK is exposed to the textiles INDUSTRY if it has lent considerably more to that industry than to others.

EXTERNAL DEBT
The financial obligations of a COMPANY or a country to overseas (that is, non-domestic) creditors.

EXTERNAL FUNDS
The FUNDS available to an ORGANISATION that come from outside the organisation, usually in the form of BANK loans, TRADE CREDIT, bonds or shares. (See also INTERNAL FUNDS.)

EXTRAORDINARY ITEM
An item in a COMPANY'S ACCOUNTS which is out of the ordinary, that is, which does not appear as a matter of course in every year's accounts. Extraordinary items need to be explained to shareholders in the company's ANNUAL REPORT.

EXTRAORDINARY RESOLUTION
A RESOLUTION, or statement of intent, to do something that falls outside a COMPANY'S ordinary course of BUSINESS. For example, a resolution to take over another company, or to dismiss a DIRECTOR for FRAUD.

FACE VALUE
The VALUE that is written on the face of a financial instrument. The face value of a SHARE (also known as the NOMINAL value, the value at which it was issued) need bear no relation to its MARKET value.

FACILITY
A service made available to customers or employees to use as and when they please. Hence an OVERDRAFT facility is a BANK overdraft made available to customers to use whenever they need it. A canteen facility is a place serving food for employees to take advantage of as they wish.

FACSIMILE
See FAX.

FACTOR
Originally, an AGENT sent from Europe by the East India Company to run its trading posts in far-flung parts of the British Empire. Today a factor is any agent who is buying and selling something on commission. (See also FACTORY and FACTORING.)

FACTORS OF PRODUCTION
The essential elements – land, LABOUR and CAPITAL – required for any wealth-creating PROCESS.

FACTORING
The business of collecting somebody else's debts on their behalf. A COMPANY sells its RECEIVABLES to a THIRD PARTY (usually a FINANCIAL INSTITUTION) at a DISCOUNT. The third party then sets out to collect the debts. Its PROFIT comes when it collects more than the discounted amount it has paid for them.

FACTORY
Originally, a trading post that was run by a FACTOR. Subsequently, any site where FACTORS OF PRODUCTION are used in the MANUFACTURE of GOODS.

FALLBACK
An alternative plan of action devised in case a primary plan fails.

Family firm
A company owned and run largely by the members of one or two families. Such firms have special characteristics and special problems, such as how to motivate non-family employees when the most senior positions in the company are probably closed to them.

Fast-moving consumer goods
See FMCG.

Fast track
There are two meanings:

- A separate career path in an organisation designed to cater for particularly able people who might not be prepared to wait and make the standard ascent of the corporate ladder.
- A procedure in the United States which allows for the fast passage of legislation concerning trade agreements.

Fax
A facsimile machine, a machine that makes paper-based copies of messages that have been transmitted electronically via telephone lines and computer networks.

FDI
See foreign direct investment.

Feasibility study
A paper-based analysis of the likelihood that a project will meet its planned targets.

Fee
A payment for the provision of professional services; for example, the lawyer's fee and the accountant's fee. Other service providers, such as window cleaners and bus conductors, are not paid fees. They are paid cash.

FIDUCIARY
Somebody (or something) that is holding assets on behalf of another person; for example, a Swiss BANK holding MONEY in trust for a CUSTOMER in another country.

FIFO
Short for first in, first out, a fundamental ACCOUNTING PRINCIPLE which says that any FUNGIBLE RAW MATERIALS being used in a BUSINESS are to be costed on the basis that the first to come in (probably the cheapest) are deemed to be the first to go out. Contrast with its opposite, LIFO.

FINAL ASSEMBLY
The last stages in an assembly PROCESS before a PRODUCT rolls off the production line.

FINANCE COMPANY
A COMPANY engaged in making loans to individuals and businesses. Unlike a BANK, a finance company does not collect deposits from RETAIL customers. Rather, it raises FUNDS by borrowing from other financial institutions and from the WHOLESALE money markets.

FINANCE DIRECTOR
The EXECUTIVE DIRECTOR on a COMPANY'S BOARD who is in charge of the company's financial position.

When my finance director weeps I know I've got my prices just right.
Franco Mancassola, chairman of cut-price airline Debonair

FINANCIAL ENGINEERING
The process of reorganising a company's finances, either by raising MONEY from one source (a BANK, say) to pay off another (TRADE creditors, perhaps); or by extending the MATURITY of the company's borrowing, raising LONG-TERM bonds, for instance, in order to repay SHORT-TERM bank loans.

Financial institution
Any COMPANY or ORGANISATION whose business is finance. This includes banks, INSURANCE companies, PENSION funds and FACTORING companies.

Financial statement
A written record of the financial position of an ORGANISATION, consisting normally of a BALANCE SHEET, an INCOME STATEMENT and a CASH FLOW statement.

Financial year
The 12-month period for which an ORGANISATION prepares its FINANCIAL STATEMENT. This may or may not coincide with the calendar year.

Finder's fee
A FEE paid to someone for bringing together two (other) parties who make a deal and do BUSINESS together. The fee may be a flat fee, or it may be calculated as a percentage of the VALUE of business arising from the MEETING.

Finished goods
GOODS which have completed the manufacturing PROCESS and are now ready to be sold to a final CONSUMER.

Fire
To bring someone's employment CONTRACT to an end, often an abrupt one.

He was fired with enthusiasm because he was not fired with enthusiasm.
Anon

Firm
Strictly speaking, a BUSINESS entity that is not incorporated; for example, a firm of lawyers who do business as a PARTNERSHIP and not as a COMPANY. The word has come to be used more widely, however, to refer to all but the largest business organisations.

FIRST IN, FIRST OUT
See FIFO.

FIRST REFUSAL
A right given by the owner of an ASSET to a potential purchaser to match anybody else's offer for that asset. Such rights are often given, either by CONTRACT or by law, to tenants of state-owned apartment blocks.

FISCAL
Of the public finances, particularly in relation to the raising and collecting of taxes.

FISCAL YEAR
The 12-month period used by governments for their accounting purposes.

FIXED ASSET
An ASSET that is used in a BUSINESS for some period of time and that is not easy to move, such as a building, land or machinery.

FIXED COST
A COST that does not vary in proportion to the amount of GOODS or SERVICES that are produced; the opposite of VARIABLE COST. Fixed costs, such as the amount paid for RENT and DEPRECIATION, are unrelated to a COMPANY'S TURNOVER. They are incurred whether it is selling a lot or a little.

FIXED RATE
An INTEREST RATE that does not vary until the financial ASSET to which it is attached comes to MATURITY. A ten-year fixed-rate LOAN has its interest rate fixed once and for all at the beginning of its ten-year life.

FLAG OF CONVENIENCE
Every ship sailing on the high seas must fly a flag to indicate where it is officially registered. A ship registered in a place with low taxes and minimum REGULATION is said to fly a flag of convenience.

Flat rate

A fixed PRICE for GOODS or SERVICES. For example, the unit price for goods is the same whether you buy 10 units or 10,000; there is no DISCOUNT for buying in bulk. Or the price charged for auditing a firm's ACCOUNTS is fixed at a flat rate, regardless of how many hours it takes.

Flexible manufacturing

A manufacturing system that can be rapidly switched from making PRODUCT A to making product B, as and when MARKET DEMAND dictates.

Flexitime

A schedule of working that allows employees to choose their working hours around a core period, usually in the middle of the day. They can thus work from 8am to 4pm if they wish, or from 10.30am to 6.30pm. Within this framework, employees have to fit a fixed number of working hours into each week. Flexitime is no good for tasks that require a team effort.

Floating charge

A CHARGE that floats over all a borrower's assets. If the borrower should fail to repay the DEBT to which the charge relates, the lender can lay claim to any of the borrowers' assets up to the value of the LOAN.

Floating rate

An INTEREST RATE that fluctuates according to MARKET rates; the opposite of FIXED RATE.

Floor

There are two BUSINESS-related meanings:

- The floor of a STOCK EXCHANGE is the physical room in which brokers transact their BUSINESS. As their business nowadays almost all takes place by telephone or computer, this sort of floor is becoming increasingly rare.
- A lower limit placed on a variable PRICE in a CONTRACT. This can be a minimum INTEREST

RATE to be paid on a FLOATING-RATE LOAN, for instance, or it can be the lowest acceptable bid on a painting at AUCTION.

Flotation
The obtaining of a QUOTATION for a COMPANY'S shares on a recognised STOCK EXCHANGE. Exchanges have extensive rules on how this can be done.

Flow chart
A diagrammatic representation of any PROCESS involving a series of steps. It may be a manufacturing process, such as the production of an automobile, or a strategic process, such as the way in which a COMPANY intends to enter a new MARKET. The flow chart will show which steps need to be taken first and which can wait until later.

Flow of funds
The ways in which MONEY moves around a COUNTRY's financial system, from banks to consumers, to producers, to government, and back to banks again.

FMCG
Short for fast-moving CONSUMER GOODS, things like foodstuffs and toothpaste that do not stay on shop shelves for long. The key to selling FMCGS profitably lies in the LOGISTICS of getting them from producer to consumer.

FOB
Short for free on board, a term attached to a PRICE QUOTATION given by an exporter. FOB signifies that the exporter undertakes, for the given price, to deliver the GOODS as far as the buyer's chosen means of transport – a port or railway station, for example. The French expression is *franco à bord*.

Focus group
A small group of consumers who are brought together for the purposes of MARKET RESEARCH, usually to discuss in some detail the merits of a particular PRODUCT or service.

Footprint
The area on the ground that is reached by a signal from a satellite. For satellite broadcasters this is their potential MARKET, the bait with which they try to entice advertisers.

Footsie
See FTSE 100.

Force majeure
A clause in a CONTRACT which abrogates the parties from responsibility in the case of events beyond their control – such as an earthquake or the outbreak of war – that prevent them from fulfilling their side of the contract.

Forced sale
Any SALE that has to take place immediately, denying the seller the opportunity to look around and wait for a better PRICE.

Forecast
An estimate of future economic or MARKET data. (See also EXTRAPOLATION.)

When in doubt, predict that the present trend will continue.
Anon

Foreign currency
The CURRENCY of a foreign country. For everybody but Americans and Puerto Ricans, the US dollar is a foreign currency.

Foreign direct investment
A substantial INVESTMENT by a resident of one country in the INDUSTRY of another. Foreign direct investment (FDI) includes all purchases of stakes of more than 10% of a foreign COMPANY, and all investment in GREENFIELD SITES abroad.

Foreign exchange
Methods of making payment from one country in

the CURRENCY of another, either electronically or by the exchange of notes and coins.

FORFAIT
The business of discounting financial instruments used to finance the export of CAPITAL GOODS. The instruments can be traded (like securities) in a SECONDARY MARKET.

FORWARD
There are at least three meanings:

- A forward CONTRACT is a contract that specifies the details of a deal to be consummated in the future, such as the SALE of wheat next September.
- Forward COVER is the buying today of the means to meet an obligation in the future.
- To forward something is to act as an intermediary by sending on to a THIRD PARTY something that you have received.

FORWARDING AGENT
A BUSINESS or an individual that arranges for the shipment of freight.

FRANCHISE
A contractual agreement in which one party (the franchisee) buys the rights from another (the franchiser) to sell GOODS and SERVICES as specified by the franchiser. McDonald's and Benetton are well-known examples of franchises.

FRAUD
An act of deception that is aimed at gaining financial benefit at the expense of others. Tinkering with companies' ACCOUNTS is a common form of fraud.

FREELANCE
Originally, a medieval mercenary who lent his lance and fighting skills to the highest bidder. Then used to refer to a journalist with no affiliation to any particular publication. Now it is used

to refer to any person who works for themselves rather than for an EMPLOYER.

FREE ON BOARD
See FOB.

FREE PORT
A port where no duties are imposed on ships that unload cargo. Free ports are designed to be places where cargoes are transferred from ship to ship, in transit to their ultimate destination.

FREE TRADE
The economic principle that optimal growth is achieved when TRADE among countries is unhindered by tariffs or invisible barriers.

FREE TRADE AREA
A region, such as the EUROPEAN UNION, where a number of national governments agree to remove any existing barriers to TRADE between them.

FREIGHT
Any GOODS that are in the process of being transported, by road, rail, sea or air.

FREIGHT FORWARDER
An AGENT who handles the shipment of EXPORTS, in particular the documentation required to get GOODS from their point of MANUFACTURE to their shipper.

FRINGE BENEFITS
Benefits that employees receive in addition to their normal WAGE or SALARY. They include such things as pensions, private health insurance, cars, low-INTEREST loans and canteen facilities. In some companies they are worth as much as one-third of a person's total REMUNERATION.

FRONT OFFICE
The opposite of the BACK OFFICE, the place where a BUSINESS has direct contact with its customers, be it a shop, a showroom, or a telephone sales operation.

FROZEN ASSETS
Assets that a court has decreed cannot be used by their owner. The freeze may be only temporary, to be removed once the reason for its imposition has gone. Assets are often frozen when the ownership of the assets is in question.

FTSE 100
The most commonly used STOCKMARKET INDEX in the UK, based on the PRICE movements of the 100 largest companies quoted on the London market. Its name is an amalgam of its two founders, the *Financial Times* and the London Stock Exchange.

FULFILMENT
The process of satisfying an ORDER received by DIRECT MAIL. Much of the fulfilment process these days is carried out by computer.

FULL EMPLOYMENT
An economy is said to have full employment when there are jobs available for every citizen who wants to work.

Don't go around saying the world owes you a living. The world owes you nothing. It was here first.
Mark Twain

FUNCTION
The work done by a self-contained part or DIVISION of a BUSINESS; for example, the marketing function or the personnel function.

FUND
Money set aside for some specific purpose, often in a TAX-advantageous way.

FUNDED
Usually seen in the phrase "fully funded", to refer to a PENSION FUND whose investments are sufficient to pay all its obligations as and when they become due. In other words, the fund does not need to rely on future contributions to meet its present obligations.

FUNDS

MONEY of any kind that is used in the running of a BUSINESS, as in FLOW OF FUNDS. Once upon a time, spelt with a capital F, Funds meant loans made by the British government.

FUNGIBLE

The quality of things, such as notes and coins or grains of sand, where any one individual specimen is indistinguishable from any other. Anything to be used as a store of VALUE (be it beads or gold coins) has to be fungible.

FUTURES

Contracts agreeing to buy something in the future for a PRICE that is fixed in the present. Futures began in agricultural markets in order to enable farmers to sell in advance crops that had not yet ripened. They have spread more recently into financial markets.

G–7
A forum for the finance ministers of the seven largest developed economies – Canada, France, Germany, Italy, Japan, the UK and the United States – to discuss economic and financial matters.

G–8
The G–7 plus Russia.

GAP ANALYSIS
A technique used by a MARKET RESEARCHER to identify gaps in a particular MARKET. Once identified, companies can set out to fill the gaps, thereby meeting unrequited CONSUMER DEMAND.

GATT
The acronym for General Agreement on Tariffs and Trade, the GATT was established in 1947. In it member countries agreed systematically to reduce the TRADE barriers between them. This was achieved in a series of rounds (the Tokyo Round, the Uruguay Round, and so on) which have taken trade liberalisation further and further. Since 1997 the GATT has been the responsibility of the WTO.

GDP
Short for gross domestic product, the sum of all output of GOODS and SERVICES produced by a nation. GNP (gross national product) is GDP plus net INCOME from abroad, (for example, the RENT and PROFIT received from other countries minus the rent and profit paid to those other countries).

Man does not live by GNP alone.
Paul Samuelson, American economist

GEARING
See DEBT-EQUITY RATIO.

GENERAL PARTNER
See LIMITED PARTNERSHIP.

GENERAL PROVISIONS
See PROVISIONS.

GENERAL STRIKE
A STRIKE involving almost all sectors of the economy. General strikes are usually organised as workers' protests against general social conditions rather than against their own specific PAY and CONTRACT.

GENERATION X
A lifestyle defined in a book of the same name. Generation Xers are, roughly, people born between 1965 and 1980, and they differ from other generations in that they are less inclined to seek full-time, lifetime employment. Instead, they prefer a series of SHORT-TERM contractual arrangements.

GENERIC
A PRODUCT that is sold with no BRAND name. Pharmaceuticals are said to become generic when they are no longer protected by PATENT and can be manufactured and sold by anybody.

GILT-EDGED
A BOND that is believed to be of exceptionally high quality (in terms of its ability to pay INTEREST and CAPITAL as and when they fall due). The term is applied particularly to British government securities, once known as gilts. (See also BLUE-CHIP.)

GLASS CEILING
The invisible barrier that prevents women from reaching the top echelons of organisations in the proportion that their numbers in BUSINESS suggest they should.

GLOBALISATION
A STRATEGY in which companies aim to sell their products and SERVICES all around the world. Driven by the convergence of CONSUMER tastes from Tbilisi to Timbuctoo, globalisation presents companies with opportunities for achieving ECONOMIES OF SCALE.

GMBH
Short for Gesellschaft mit beschrankte Haftung, a German form of incorporation roughly equivalent to a LIMITED LIABILITY COMPANY.

GNP
Gross national product (see GDP).

GOING CONCERN
An assumption made by an ACCOUNTANT when preparing a COMPANY'S BOOKS that the company is going to continue in BUSINESS for the foreseeable future. If this assumption were not made the company's assets would have to be valued at the (low) PRICE that they would realise in a FORCED SALE.

GOLD FIXING
A twice-daily agreement among the biggest dealers in the gold MARKET as to what the market PRICE of the precious metal should be. This was an important event when governments pegged their currencies to a fixed amount of gold (the days of the so-called gold standard). It is not so any more.

GOLD CARD
A CREDIT CARD or CHARGE CARD with a number of special privileges (such as a higher credit limit) that are not granted to the holders of ungilded cards.

GOLD CLAUSE
A clause in a LOAN agreement that relates the borrower's repayment to the VALUE of a fixed volume of gold. Such clauses appear in times of high INFLATION and when the PRICE of gold is stable.

GOLD STANDARD
See GOLD FIXING.

GOLDEN HANDCUFFS
The terms of an employment CONTRACT designed to deter a key EMPLOYEE from leaving. A STOCK OPTION which is forfeited (or which has to be realised when the employee leaves) is one form of golden handcuff.

Golden handshake
A generous upfront payment designed to persuade a person to leave their current employment and to join the ORGANISATION offering the payment.

Golden parachute
A clause written into the CONTRACT of senior employees guaranteeing them a generous payment if they should lose their job for any reason, or be downgraded. Golden parachutes provide protection to senior executives in the case of a TAKEOVER. They also discourage new owners from laying off the existing MANAGEMENT and replacing them with their own employees.

Golden share
A SHARE which gives the holder special rights, in particular the right of veto when there is a TAKEOVER BID for the COMPANY. Governments often like to retain such shares when privatising sensitive industries, such as telecoms or defence.

Good faith
The principle of acting reasonably and honestly. In many countries there is a legal duty for all parties to agreements to act in good faith.

Goods
Movable property manufactured for the purpose of being sold to customers.

We are not here to sell a parcel of boilers and vats, but the potentiality of growing rich beyond the dreams of avarice.
Dr Johnson

Goodwill
An accounting term for the difference between the amount that a COMPANY pays for another company and the MARKET VALUE of the other company's assets. Goodwill is thus an INTANGIBLE ASSET representing things like the value of the company's BRAND names and the skills of its employees.

GOVERNANCE
The form and style in which a COMPANY is governed, by the law, by its own statutes and by custom. This can vary greatly from country to country. The roles of the state in France, of banks in Germany and of shareholders in the United States in the governance of corporations are uniquely powerful.

GRACE PERIOD
The time between the granting of a LOAN and the first repayment. It is also the amount of time allowed by a loan or INSURANCE CONTRACT between an overdue payment and cancellation of the contract.

GRANDFATHER CLAUSE
A clause in an agreement (especially in the GATT) which allows the parties to the agreement to exempt certain things that were in existence in their own laws before the agreement was reached.

GRANT
MONEY provided for a BUSINESS project from outside normal commercial sources. For example, a government grant that is given to encourage a COMPANY to build a new FACTORY in a particular place.

GREENFIELD SITE
A previously agricultural site outside an urban area on which a COMPANY builds a FACTORY or OFFICE. (See also BROWNFIELD SITE.)

GREENMAIL
When someone acquires a large shareholding in a COMPANY with the aim of getting the company to buy the shares back at a higher price by pretending they were bought as part of a plan to take over the company.

GREY MARKET
A MARKET for trading in shares not yet issued; before a new ISSUE has been allocated to investors the shares are traded on a basis of "when issued", denoted by the letters WI.

Gross
The total amount of something – gross sales, gross PROFIT, and so on – before taking into account a number of costs, such as TAX or DEPRECIATION.

My problem lies in reconciling my gross habits with my net profit.
Errol Flynn

Group
A number of companies which are owned by each other or by a common HOLDING COMPANY. Most groups consist of a PARENT COMPANY and several subsidiaries.

Group accounts
The ACCOUNTS of a GROUP in which all transactions between members of the group are netted out. So the group's sales, for example, are less than the sum of the sales of the individual companies within the group, assuming that at least one of them has sold something to one of the others.

Group of Eight
See G–8.

Group of seven
See G–7.

Groupware
A SOFTWARE PROGRAM which links people with a common interest and enables them to communicate rapidly and easily with each other.

Growth
An increase in some measure or other of a COMPANY'S performance between one ACCOUNTING PERIOD and another, most often the increase in the VALUE of either its sales or its PROFIT. A country's economic growth rate is the percentage by which its GDP changes over a given period, usually a year.

GSM

Short for global system for mobile, a telecommunications project that aims to link national mobile phone systems in a way that will enable customers to call around the world with their mobile phones as easily as they do with fixed-line phones.

GSP

Short for generalised system of preferences, an agreement among developed countries that they will give preferential treatment to certain IMPORTS from developing countries. The GSP allows countries to break the no favouritism rules of the GATT.

GUARANTEE

An undertaking by someone that they will be responsible for an obligation (a DEBT or a promise of good behaviour) if the person who is bound by the obligation fails to fulfil it. To be binding in court, a guarantee needs to be made in writing.

Guarantees are often given by manufacturers, promising consumers that their GOODS will meet certain standards for a certain length of time. These days, however, such promises often provide little more protection to consumers than the ordinary law of the land.

I reject the term guru because it is associated with pandering to the masses, providing inspiration without substance. There is a little bit of the shaman in a guru.

Rosabeth Moss Kanter

GURU

A BUSINESS academic or MANAGEMENT CONSULTANT who is known for his or her expertise in a particular business area. Gurus are much in demand in the MEDIA.

HACK
To gain unauthorised access into somebody's computer system from a computer outside it.

HACKER
A person, often young, who is skilled at gaining unauthorised access into other people's computer systems.

HARD CURRENCY
A CURRENCY that does not normally depreciate (that is, lose its VALUE) against other currencies over time. For this reason hard currencies – the US dollar, the D-mark and the Swiss franc – are favoured for denominating international TRADE. The EURO is widely expected to become a hard currency to rival the dollar.

HARDWARE
The bits and pieces of any computer system that can be kicked, that is, they take up physical space. The opposite of SOFTWARE.

HARD SELL
An exceptionally forceful attempt by a SALESMAN to sell GOODS OR SERVICES to a CONSUMER. A hard sell can backfire if it intimidates the consumer to such an extent that it puts him off making a purchase.

Everyone lives by selling something.
Robert Louis Stevenson

HEADHUNTER
A person or a FIRM employed by a COMPANY to help recruit someone to fill a senior post, usually by persuading skilled employees elsewhere to change jobs. Headhunters are more pompously known as EXECUTIVE search consultants.

HEADQUARTERS
The place where a COMPANY's senior executives have their offices and where its BOARD holds its meetings. It may or may not be the officially reg-

istered address of the company.

Heavy industry
An INDUSTRY which produces heavy GOODS and uses heavy equipment to do it. Examples are the steel, automobile and shipbuilding industries, which are both LABOUR INTENSIVE and CAPITAL INTENSIVE. The opposite of LIGHT INDUSTRY.

Hedge
A means of reducing the RISK of LOSS from future PRICE movements. Owning property is said to be a good hedge against the reduction in the VALUE of MONEY that occurs at a time of INFLATION. International businesses seek to hedge against the risk from movements in FOREIGN-EXCHANGE markets. Those that do not have on occasions lost out badly.

Hidden agenda
The undisclosed objectives that a person has, usually when participating in a MEETING.

Hidden reserves
The reserves of a COMPANY that are not disclosed in its BALANCE SHEET. These may arise from an undervaluation of its assets or from hidden BANK accounts (abroad).

High tech
Short for high technology, modern advances in science that have found industrial and commercial uses. Often associated with developments in INFORMATION TECHNOLOGY.

Any technology sufficiently advanced is indistinguishable from magic.
Arthur C. Clarke

Historic cost
The COST of an ASSET on the day that it was purchased; its original cost. Contrast with REPLACEMENT COST. In the United States it is known as historical cost.

Hoarding
See BILLBOARD.

Holding company
A COMPANY which exists almost solely for the purpose of holding (that is, owning) shares in other companies.

Home page
The opening screen on an ORGANISATION'S WEB SITE. The home page usually offers a directory to guide the reader to other parts of the site. It is the screen to which the reader is returned if lost.

Home worker
A person who works from home using some basic sort of equipment, for example, a computer, a telephone or a knitting machine. (See also OUTWORKER and SOHO.)

Horizontal integration
The integration of companies that are in more or less the same line of business. Daimler-Benz merging with Chrysler is a case of horizontal integration; Daimler-Benz getting into the defence INDUSTRY is not. (See also VERTICAL INTEGRATION.)

Hostile takeover
A TAKEOVER in which the COMPANY being taken over does not wish to be bought. A company subject to such an offer sets about resisting it or finding an alternative. (See also WHITE KNIGHT.)

Hot money
CAPITAL with no allegiance to any particular MARKET. It flows rapidly and frequently across borders in search of nothing more than the highest SHORT-TERM RETURN. Hot money may also be moving rapidly because it is being chased by TAX inspectors or FRAUD investigators.

Human resources
The people who make up the WORKFORCE of an ORGANISATION with their various strengths and

weaknesses. Human-resource MANAGEMENT is concerned with getting the best out of these resources for the benefit of the organisation.

How come when I want a pair of hands I get a human being as well?
Henry Ford

HURDLE RATE
The RATE OF RETURN that has to be achieved by an INVESTMENT for it to be considered a success. This may be its cost of FUNDS, or it may be the RETURN on EQUITY (ROE) achieved by other firms in the same INDUSTRY.

HYPERINFLATION
A level of INFLATION that is so extraordinarily high that paper MONEY becomes worthless almost overnight. Under such conditions, with no recognisable store of VALUE, it is virtually impossible to do BUSINESS in conventional ways.

ICC

Short for International Chamber of Commerce, a Paris-based ORGANISATION that acts as the international forum for national chambers of commerce. The ICC also acts as an ARBITRATOR in many international TRADE disputes.

ICON

A small graphic motif on a computer screen that directs the user to a SOFTWARE PROGRAM.

IDLE CAPACITY

Industrial CAPACITY that is lying idle for some reason, such as a shortage of RAW MATERIALS or LABOUR, or a lack of orders.

IMF

Short for International Monetary Fund, a FINANCIAL INSTITUTION set up by the BRETTON WOODS agreement. The IMF was designed to enable member countries to borrow from each other in order to iron out irregularities in their exchange rates and RESERVES. Countries are required to meet strict economic and financial conditions if they want to become borrowers.

IMPORTS

GOODS or SERVICES that are bought by someone or some organisation in a country other than the one in which they are produced.

IMPULSE BUYING

The purchase of GOODS on impulse; buying something because it has been seen in a shop window rather than because of a predetermined need for it. We buy chocolates on impulse; but rarely diamonds.

IN-HOUSE

Within the COMPANY or ORGANISATION. Doing something in-house means that it is being done by somebody on the company's PAYROLL rather than by an outsider. The opposite of OUTSOURCING.

IN PLAY
An expression used to refer to a QUOTED COMPANY that is known to be vulnerable to a contested TAKEOVER.

INC
See INCORPORATION.

INCENTIVE
A promised reward that motivates an EMPLOYEE to work harder and be more productive. An incentive BONUS is a payment made for production that is in excess of an agreed amount.

INCOME
The monetary reward that comes from the productive use of land, LABOUR and/or CAPITAL.

INCOME STATEMENT
Called the PROFIT AND LOSS ACCOUNT in the UK, this is the US term for the accounting statement that shows an ORGANISATION'S REVENUE and its COSTS over a period (usually the organisation's FINANCIAL YEAR), and its resulting PROFIT or LOSS

INCOME TAX
A TAX imposed on individuals or businesses and calculated as a proportion of their INCOME. For most governments it is the largest REVENUE-earner of all taxes.

INCORPORATION
The process of obtaining the approval of the authorities to organise and run a corporation. In the United States an ORGANISATION that is incorporated must include the letters Inc after its name.

INDEMNITY
An agreement to compensate someone for a specified type of LOSS, should one occur.

INDEMNITY INSURANCE
See D&O.

INDEX

A way of comparing disparate things (often their prices) related to an earlier base period, which is often given the value of 100. The things may be CONSUMER GOODS (as in the CONSUMER PRICE INDEX) or stocks and shares (as in the STOCKMARKET index). See also DOW JONES and FTSE 100.

INDEXATION

The process of linking the COST or PRICE of something to an INDEX. Wages that move in line with the CONSUMER PRICE INDEX (to enable them to take account of generally rising prices, that is, INFLATION) are said to be indexed.

INDIRECT COST

The costs involved in manufacturing or in providing a service which cannot be attributed to a particular PRODUCT or service. The COST of the electricity required to heat a COMPANY'S HEADQUARTERS, or the premiums paid to insure factories against fire damage, are both examples of indirect costs. An indirect cost is also known as an overhead.

INDIRECT TAXATION

A TAX that is not imposed directly on an individual or ORGANISATION. For example, VAT in Europe or sales tax in the United States, which are levied on the TURNOVER of a PRODUCT. Also customs DUTY, which is an AD VALOREM tax on imported GOODS.

INDUCTION

A formalised way of introducing someone to a new place of work. An induction course can include lectures about the history of the COMPANY, a guided tour of its PREMISES and visits to customers.

INDUSTRIAL RELATIONS

The relations between employers, employees, trade unions and government.

INDUSTRIALISATION

The process of becoming an economy that is

based on INDUSTRY: one with a large number of factories involved in manufacturing GOODS.

INDUSTRY
A SECTOR of the BUSINESS world, such as manufacturing industry or the steel industry. Also all these sectors taken together.

INFLATION
An increase over time in the prices of GOODS and SERVICES. Inflation is usually measured by the CONSUMER PRICE INDEX, a basket of the goods and services bought by the average householder.

INFLATION ACCOUNTING
A way of coping with INFLATION when preparing a COMPANY'S ACCOUNTS; a way of addressing the fact that the dollar that bought something at the beginning of the year is not worth the same as the dollar that it was sold for at the end of the year. On paper it could look as if there was no LOSS on the purchase and SALE, but that would be misleading.

INFORMATION TECHNOLOGY
The technologies that enable the rapid and widespread dissemination of information, essentially the technology of the computer and the telephone, and the interplay between them. Frequently abbreviated to IT.

INFRASTRUCTURE
The basic PLANT and SERVICES underpinning the operation of a BUSINESS or of a country.

You and I come by road or rail. But economists travel on infrastructure.
Margaret Thatcher

INJUNCTION
A legal measure to restrain someone from doing something on the grounds that it may, for example, cause injury or inequity.

INNOVATION

The addition of new elements to products and SERVICES, or to the methods of producing and MARKETING them. Innovation is a continuous process of adding improvements at the margin. It is not the same as invention, which involves an element of sudden and dramatic discovery.

Innovation is 1% inspiration and 99% perspiration.
Thomas Edison

INSIDE INFORMATION

Information which is received because the recipient is in a privileged position. Thus an INVESTMENT banker working on a TAKEOVER will know about it before the general public, and so will the directors of the COMPANY doing the taking over. They would all be deemed to be in possession of inside information.

INSIDER

A person who is in possession of INSIDE INFORMATION.

INSIDER DEALING

Dealing in stocks and shares on the basis of INSIDE INFORMATION. In many developed countries this is illegal. Although hard to prove, a few people have served time in prison for it.

INSOLVENCY

The state of a COMPANY that is unable to pay its debts on time. If the company can manage to RESCHEDULE its debts before any of its debtors press their claims through the courts, it may avoid going into LIQUIDATION.

INSTALMENT CREDIT

A LOAN provided for the purchase of CONSUMER GOODS which is repaid in a number of regular equal instalments over an agreed period of time.

INSTITUTIONAL INVESTOR
Any ORGANISATION that trades securities in large volumes over a long period of time; for example, PENSION funds, INSURANCE companies and INVESTMENT banks. The market behaviour of institutional investors is very different from that of RETAIL investors.

INSURANCE
A CONTRACT between one party (the insurer) and another (the insured) in which the insurer agrees to reimburse the insured for defined losses over a defined period of time. This is called casualty insurance to differentiate it from life ASSURANCE.

Insurance is like fun. The older you get the more it costs.
Frank Hubbard

INSURANCE PREMIUM
A payment made to obtain INSURANCE.

INTANGIBLE ASSET
A BUSINESS ASSET which cannot be kicked, such as GOODWILL, a BRAND name, or the inventiveness of a COMPANY'S R&D department. Intangibles obviously have considerable VALUE, but it is hard for an ACCOUNTANT to put a number on it.

INTEGRATION
See VERTICAL and HORIZONTAL INTEGRATION.

INTELLECTUAL PROPERTY
Ideas, designs or inventions – the fruits of the intellect. By means of a PATENT, a TRADEMARK and COPYRIGHT law, intellectual property can be protected from commercial exploitation by copycats. It can also be bought and sold like REAL ESTATE.

INTERACTIVE
Any means of communication between two parties in which both parties can communicate simultaneously with each other. So the telephone is interactive, but the television is not (yet).

INTERBANK RATE
The RATE OF INTEREST that banks charge each other for borrowing and lending MONEY among themselves.

INTEREST
There are two BUSINESS-related meanings:

- The MONEY paid for the privilege of borrowing money.
- A share in an ASSET. For example: "They had a 50% interest in the building."

INTEREST COVER
The number of times a COMPANY can COVER (out of profits) the COST of the INTEREST payments it has to make on loans. In other words, PROFIT over the year (before interest and TAX) divided by the amount of interest paid out over the same period. The lower the interest cover, the lower is the likelihood that a company will be able to pay its shareholders a DIVIDEND.

INTEREST RATE
The amount charged for borrowing MONEY for a year, expressed as a percentage of the amount borrowed.

INTERFACE
The HARDWARE and SOFTWARE that lie between two computers and that allow them to communicate with each other. From this specialist meaning the word has come to be used for any bridge that connects things, people or ideas.

INTERIM ACCOUNTS
ACCOUNTS produced somewhere between the beginning and the end of a COMPANY'S FINANCIAL YEAR. Some stock exchanges demand that quoted companies produce interim accounts six months after their full-year accounts. Banks may demand that companies produce interim accounts to support a request for a LOAN.

INTERIM DIVIDEND
Part of a COMPANY's annual DIVIDEND that is paid in stages (usually six-monthly or three-monthly) during the year.

INTERIM MANAGER
A manager who is employed by a COMPANY at a senior level for only a short period of time. An interim manager's job usually focuses on sorting out a particular problem or seeing through a particular STRATEGY or course of action. (See also TROUBLESHOOTER.)

INTERMEDIARY
Any ORGANISATION or individual that acts as a go-between.

INTERMEDIATE GOODS
GOODS which lie somewhere on the production line between RAW MATERIALS and finished products. Rolls of steel, for example, are intermediate goods in the MANUFACTURE of cars. Iron ore is the raw material; the car is the finished PRODUCT.

INTERMEDIATE TECHNOLOGY
Technology which is appropriate to the state of development of a country or an INDUSTRY, particularly used with reference to developing countries that are not at the frontier of technical knowledge. For example, encouraging the use of handicraft skills and tools for the manufacture of furniture in central Africa, rather than investing in high-tech factories full of robots.

INTERMEDIATION
The addition of new intermediaries into a BUSINESS PROCESS. (See also DISINTERMEDIATION.)

INTERMODAL
The use of several different modes of transport (road, rail, sea or air) to ship GOODS from one place to another.

INTERNAL FUNDS
FUNDS which a COMPANY generates from its own efforts. These are available to be paid out as dividends to shareholders or for INVESTMENT. Compare with EXTERNAL FUNDS.

INTERNAL RATE OF RETURN
The rate at which a future CASH FLOW has to be discounted to give an amount exactly equal to the INVESTMENT in the project. If the internal rate of return (IRR) is higher than the INTEREST that could be earned from leaving the MONEY in a BANK, then the project would appear to be a reasonable one.

INTERNATIONAL
Anything that is carried on between two or more different nations. (See also MULTINATIONAL and TRANSNATIONAL.)

INTERNET
A worldwide NETWORK of interlinked computers that can be accessed by anybody with a personal computer and a modem. The Internet is used to disseminate information (via the WORLD WIDE WEB), to send messages (by E-MAIL), and to enable groups with common interests to communicate.

INTERVIEW
A MEETING between people for the purpose of exchanging information with a view (most frequently) to giving one of the people a job, or to writing an article about them.

INTRANET
A NETWORK of computer links set up within an ORGANISATION to enable the members of that organisation to communicate (exclusively) with each other. An intranet may also have a link to the INTERNET and the outside world.

INVENTORY
The inputs a COMPANY holds that are necessary for its production processes plus the unsold FINISHED GOODS that it holds in its WAREHOUSE or wherever.

In the UK the term used is STOCK.

INVESTMENT
The purchase of a CAPITAL ASSET with the intention of gaining an INCOME from it or of making a CAPITAL GAIN. Buying stocks and shares is investment, so too is buying property for RENT or a COMPANY for its profits. By and large, buying jewellery is not an investment.

INVESTMENT APPRAISAL
The process of determining the likely RATE OF RETURN of an INVESTMENT.

INVESTMENT BANK
A BANK which specialises in providing companies with advice on how to raise MONEY to fund their INVESTMENT plans. Much of this advice relates to MERGERS AND ACQUISITIONS. In general, investment banks do not lend money themselves. But they do organise the ISSUE and SALE of securities on behalf of their corporate clients.

INVESTMENT GRADE
The rating that a SECURITY needs to obtain from CREDIT-RATING agencies if institutional investors are to be allowed (by their statutes) to buy it.

INVESTMENT GRANT
A GRANT given for the purpose of INVESTMENT.

INVESTOR
An ORGANISATION or an individual who makes an INVESTMENT.

INVESTOR RELATIONS
That part of a COMPANY's activity designed to maintain good relations with its shareholders.

INVISIBLES
Traded items that never see the inside of a container, such as banking SERVICES, tourism and SOFTWARE design.

Invoice
A document prepared by a seller of goods and sent to the buyer demanding payment. (See also pro forma.)

Invoice discounting
The selling of a company's invoices to a financial firm at a discount to their face value. Companies do this to improve their cash flow. (See also factoring.)

IPO
Short for initial public offering, the first offering of a company's securities to the general public.

IRR
See internal rate of return

ISDN
Short for Integrated Services Digital Network, a telecommunications technology that promises to revolutionise the way in which voice and data communications are transmitted.

ISO
Short for International Standards Organisation, an association of almost 100 countries that tries to standardise technical and industrial processes. It publishes a series of International Standards which recommend a minimum quality and/or performance for manufactured goods.

Issue
A large block of securities that are sold all together at one go.

IT
See information technology.

Itemised billing
Invoices for things like telephone calls that are broken down item-by-item. Computerised analysis allows customers to receive details of each call to which the invoice relates.

JIT
The ACRONYM for just in time, a Japanese MANAGEMENT system based on the principle that no STOCK should arrive for processing until the minute that it is actually required. JIT saves large sums of money by eliminating unnecessary INVENTORY, but it requires highly sophisticated LOGISTICS systems to operate properly.

JOB DESCRIPTION
A formal written description of a job, laying down all that is expected of the person who is employed to do that job.

JOB EVALUATION
A regular, systematic process in which employees' performances in their jobs are assessed by senior managers. The assessment includes recommendations about TRAINING and individual development.

JOB LOT
A collection of miscellaneous GOODS of uncertain VALUE. The goods may, for example, have been soiled in a fire or be past their sell-by date.

JOB SPECIFICATION
A detailed description of the qualifications, skills and experience required to do a particular job.

JOB SECURITY
The extent to which there is a risk of REDUNDANCY attached to a particular job, or the extent to which an EMPLOYEE believes that there is such a risk.

JOB SHARING
The division of one job between two or more part-time employees. Job sharing particularly suits jobs which involve serving a list of clients, such as home nursing.

JOBBING
A system of production used when the quantity of GOODS to be manufactured is too small to justify the cost of setting up a system of MASS PRODUCTION.

JOINT LIABILITY
A type of LIABILITY which is the responsibility of a whole group of people (a GUARANTEE of a BANK LOAN to a COMPANY that has been signed by all the company's directors, for example). Anyone wishing to take legal action for the liability must sue the group as a whole.

JOINT AND SEVERAL LIABILITY
A LIABILITY which is the responsibility of a group of people and for which the people can be sued either jointly or individually. (See JOINT LIABILITY and SEVERAL LIABILITY.)

JOINT STOCK COMPANY
A company that is owned jointly by its stockholders, that is, its shareholders.

JOINT VENTURE
A project entered into jointly by two or more parties. Often the parties set up a separate COMPANY to operate the venture. It usually has a specific purpose and a finite (shortish) life.

JUNIOR DEBT
See SENIOR DEBT.

JUNK BOND
A BOND issued by a COMPANY in the United States whose CREDIT RATING (from a CREDIT-RATING AGENCY) is below the so-called INVESTMENT GRADE. A number of American financial institutions (such as PENSION funds and INSURANCE companies) are legally forbidden to purchase securities that have a rating below investment grade.

More generally, a junk bond is any bond issued by a company (or a country) whose reputation for prompt repayment is less than spotless.

JUNK MAIL
Unsolicited promotional and ADVERTISING material that is delivered by mail. Increasingly, the expression embraces such mail delivered electronically, as well as by the postman.

Kaizen

See CONTINUOUS IMPROVEMENT.

Keiretsu

A type of corporate STRUCTURE found in Japan in which a large number of companies own small stakes in each other. These companies work together in a vertically integrated chain that provides everything from the RAW MATERIALS to the CONSUMER CREDIT that enables the final CONSUMER to buy the *keiretsu*'s finished products. The *keiretsu* model has aroused much interest in the West.

Key money

MONEY that has to be paid in advance as a DEPOSIT to secure a rented property.

Key person

A senior EXECUTIVE in a COMPANY whose life and/or health is insured by the company. If the person should die or be ill within a certain period the company receives COMPENSATION from the insurer.

Keyword

The words, or sequence of symbols, that are fed into the SEARCH ENGINE of an electronic DATABASE to extract specific information. The care given to selecting keywords determines the relevance of the information retrieved.

Kickback

A payment made to an individual who is responsible for awarding a CONTRACT (or for making a purchase) to persuade them to award it in favour of the payer of the kickback. In most circumstances kickbacks are illegal.

Behind every great fortune there is a crime.

Honoré de Balzac

Know-how

A special technique or skill which a COMPANY has developed and which has a VALUE to that company, either because it gives it a COMPETITIVE ADVANTAGE over its rivals, or because it can sell the skill or technique to others.

KNOWLEDGE MANAGEMENT
The process of managing the knowledge that a company owns, either collectively, through such things as its patents and KNOW-HOW, or individually in the minds of its employees. More and more companies are appointing knowledge-management officers to be in charge of this FUNCTION.

From now on the key is knowledge. The world is becoming not labour intensive, not materials intensive, not energy intensive, but knowledge intensive.
Peter Drucker

KOKUSAIKA
The Japanese word for internationalisation, something that is interpreted as the spread of Japanese corporations around the rest of the world rather than the spread of the rest of the world's corporations around Japan.

LABOUR
Human effort: one of the three FACTORS OF PRODUCTION at the root of all studies of ECONOMICS. The other two are land and CAPITAL.

LABOUR FORCE
See WORKFORCE.

LABOUR INTENSIVE
A description of products or SERVICES that require a high input of LABOUR compared with the amount of land and CAPITAL. Postal services and catering are labour intensive; flying planes and making steel (these days) are not.

LABOUR MOBILITY
The willingness of workers to move from one place to another in pursuit of a new job.

LABOUR RELATIONS
See INDUSTRIAL RELATIONS.

LAISSEZ FAIRE
French for "let it happen", an expression used to refer to a particular sort of free-MARKET ECONOMICS in which government interference with pure market forces is kept to a minimum.

LAN
The ACRONYM for local area network, a computer NETWORK that embraces a number of computers whose workers have a common interest: for example, they all work in one particular building, or they all work at one particular FUNCTION (accounting, say).

LANDED
A term used to refer to a shipment of GOODS at the time and place when and where they are delivered.

LANDLORD
A COMPANY or an individual who receives INCOME from tenants making use of land and property

over which the company or individual has the rights.

Laptop computer
A type of computer that can be used on the lap. Laptop computers have their own internal batteries which can be recharged and run independently of the mains. The smallest type of laptop is sometimes called a NOTEBOOK COMPUTER.

Laser printer
A printer which uses a laser beam to generate an image of whatever is to be printed. Laser printers are used in conjunction with computers to print out electronically-stored data.

Last in first out
See LIFO.

Launch
The introduction of a new PRODUCT or service into a MARKET. This usually involves a co-ordinated ADVERTISING CAMPAIGN and intensive DISTRIBUTION.

Launder
To pass "dirty" MONEY through "clean" places, such as reputable financial centres, so that the money appears to have been acquired legitimately, or to have had any TAX due on it paid in full.

Law of diminishing returns
The economic principle that, after a certain level of production, the same input produces a diminishing amount of output. This can be because of diseconomies of scale: as things get bigger they may require more MANAGEMENT input to produce the same output.

Lawyer's letter
The initial shot in a potential legal battle. A letter, for instance, sent by a lawyer to an intransigent DEBTOR demanding payment within a certain time.

Lay off
To end somebody's employment, either temporarily or permanently, because of cuts by the employing ORGANISATION. A temporary slowdown in DEMAND for cars, for instance, might lead a car manufacturer to lay off some of its production workers for a few months, until demand picks up again.

LBO
Short for leveraged buy-out, a TAKEOVER of a COMPANY in which most of the purchase PRICE is paid with borrowed MONEY, which (usually) then becomes a LIABILITY of the company that has been purchased.

Lead time
The amount of time between the placing of an ORDER and the actual receipt of the GOODS that have been ordered. Lead times are an important variable in the planning of production processes.

People prefer being led to being managed.
Sir Peter Parker, British businessman

Leadership
A human quality that makes people prepared to follow one person but not another. Some maintain that people are born with leadership; others maintain that it can be learnt.

Either lead, follow or get out of the way.
Ted Turner, founder of CNN

Lean production
A term used to refer to a particular method of production devised by Japanese manufacturers in their efforts in the 1960s and 1970s to catch up with their western counterparts. It involved minimising production costs as much as possible, and wherever possible.

LEARNING ORGANISATION
The type of ORGANISATION that makes a systematic attempt to retain and redistribute in an optimum way the information and knowledge that it gathers in its day-to-day business.

LEASE
A CONTRACT granting the right to the use of property for a given period of time and for a given payment (or series of payments). If the property is land or buildings, the payment is called RENT. (See also LESSEE and LESSOR.)

LEASE BACK
An arrangement under which an ORGANISATION which owns land or buildings sells them to a financial intermediary and immediately leases them back from the intermediary. This can have a dramatic effect on the organisation's BALANCE SHEET.

LEASING
The hiring (by a manufacturer) of large CAPITAL assets (such as machinery) from a financial intermediary. Leasing enables the LESSEE to exchange what would have been a single large capital payment for a series of instalments that can be considered as an EXPENSE paid out of INCOME. This can produce TAX benefits for both the LESSOR and the lessee.

LEDGER
A book in which an ORGANISATION'S ACCOUNTS are formally recorded.

LEGAL TENDER
Any sort of MONEY which is a legally acceptable form for paying a DEBT. Notes and coins are legal tender. Cheques and credit cards are not, since a vendor or a lender is not obliged to accept them as payment.

LESSEE
An individual or ORGANISATION to whom a LEASE is granted.

LESSOR
An individual or ORGANISATION who grants a LEASE to another individual or organisation.

LETTER OF CREDIT
An arrangement whereby a BANK makes FUNDS available to a CUSTOMER in a foreign country. The bank debits the customer's account at the same time as it sends a letter to a suitable bank abroad asking it to give the customer CREDIT. A letter of credit (L/C) is useful for the finance of TRADE as well as of foreign travel. The bank abroad will usually have a continuing agreement with the home bank to provide this service for its customers. Such a bank is called the home bank's correspondent.

LETTER OF INTENT
A letter formally expressing an intention to take a particular course of action. A letter of intent is not legally binding providing it is written in a way that makes it clear that it is intended not to be; it merely indicates that something is being contemplated.

LEVERAGE
See DEBT-EQUITY RATIO.

LEVERAGED BUY-OUT
See LBO.

LIABILITY
There are at least three meanings:

- An amount of MONEY that is owed.
- An obligation to do something in the future.
- The legal responsibility for DAMAGES for BREACH of CONTRACT or some other civil wrong.

LICENCE
A right granted by one ORGANISATION to another to use a PROCESS, TRADEMARK, PATENT, and so on, belonging to the first organisation in return for a FEE, or for the payment of a ROYALTY.

LICENSEE
An individual or ORGANISATION to whom a LICENCE is granted.

LICENSING
A method of expanding a business by granting licences to independent organisations in other markets (particularly markets abroad).

LICENSOR
An individual or ORGANISATION who grants a LICENCE to somebody else.

LIFE ASSURANCE
See ASSURANCE.

LIFETIME EMPLOYMENT
The practice of working for the same EMPLOYER from the moment that a person enters the WORKFORCE to the day that they retire. Lifetime employment is increasingly rare, but immediately after the second world war it was commonplace.

LIFO
The ACRONYM for last in first out, an ACCOUNTING PRINCIPLE whereby (for valuation purposes) the last STOCK-in-trade that was purchased is considered to be the first to be consumed in the production PROCESS. (See also FIFO.)

LIMITED LIABILITY
The fundamental principle of incorporation whereby a so-called limited COMPANY is limited in its obligations to the amount of EQUITY that is raised by its shareholders. A CREDITOR of a limited liability company does not have legal recourse to the directors or the individual shareholders *per se* for payment of the company's debts. (See also LTD.)

LIMITED PARTNERSHIP
A form of PARTNERSHIP in which one or more of the partners run the partnership (and have unlimited LIABILITY) and a number of other partners con-

tribute only CAPITAL to the partnership (and have their liability limited to the amount of capital that they invest). The partners with unlimited liability are called general partners; those with limited liability are called limited partners. The limited partners have no right to participate in the running of the BUSINESS.

LINE EXTENSION

A MARKETING term for the increase in a PRODUCT LINE brought about by adding variations of an existing BRAND; for example, by adding to a brand of chocolate bars like Mars a brand of Mars ice-cream.

LINE MANAGEMENT

The managers responsible for the actual production of an ORGANISATION'S GOODS and SERVICES. The expression comes from the military where line duties are those involved directly in the line of fighting, whereas STAFF duties are associated with the HEADQUARTERS and support functions.

LINE OF CREDIT

See CREDIT LINE.

LIQUIDATION

The process of redistributing a COMPANY'S assets after it has ceased trading. The company may have ceased trading of its own volition, in which case the process is called voluntary liquidation, or it may have ceased trading on the instructions of a court because it has failed to meet its obligations on time.

Failures are like skinned knees – painful but superficial.
H. Ross Perot, founder of EDS

LIQUIDITY

A measure of how quickly a COMPANY (or a MARKET) can turn its assets into CASH. A BANK is highly liquid compared with a hotel company, for instance.

Financial institutions like banks have to maintain a certain level of liquidity (imposed by their regulators) so that they can pay out their depositors' MONEY easily should there be a (temporary) loss of confidence in the institution.

LIST PRICE
The formal PRICE of GOODS and SERVICES as recorded on a list produced by the manufacturer or service provider. This may not be the price that customers are actually asked to pay. (See VOLUME DISCOUNT.)

LISTING
The adding of a COMPANY's securities to the list of those that are traded on a recognised STOCK EXCHANGE.

LISTING REQUIREMENTS
The things that a COMPANY is obliged to do before its securities can obtain a LISTING on a STOCK EXCHANGE. These usually include:

- being in BUSINESS for a minimum length of time;
- making a PROFIT for a certain period; and
- producing ACCOUNTS prepared according to the stock exchange's own requirements, which may demand DISCLOSURE well beyond what is required by the law of the land.

LLOYD'S
A unique London-based INSURANCE MARKET that began in the 18th century in the coffee shop of a man named Edward Lloyd. The market is known particularly for insuring marine risks, but it suffered a series of heavy losses in the 1980s when it went into BUSINESS with which it was less familiar.

LOAD
To put a SOFTWARE PROGRAM or a quantity of data into a computer. (See also DOWNLOAD.)

LOAD FACTOR
The percentage of a carrier's capacity that is occupied. For example, an airline may need, on average, a load factor of 75% – ie to sell more than 75% of its seats in order to be profitable.

LOAN
A transaction in which the owner of property (the lender) allows another person (the borrower) to have use of that property, usually for an agreed time and for an agreed PRICE. The property in question, of course, is (more often than not) MONEY.

LOAN STOCK
That part of a COMPANY'S CAPITAL which is in the form of LONG-TERM loans or bonds.

LOCAL AREA NETWORK
See LAN.

LOCK-OUT
The exclusion from a place of work (an OFFICE or a FACTORY) of one group of workers by another. Lock-outs usually occur as part of an industrial dispute between trade unions and managers.

LOG ON
To go through the stages required to gain access to the programs and information contained within a computer.

LOGISTICS
A term taken from the military where it referred to the science of supplying and moving troops; hence the science of moving GOODS, SERVICES and people in and out of corporations.

LOGO
The design or symbol that uniquely identifies a particular ORGANISATION or BRAND.

LONG
An INVESTOR is said to be long in a STOCK when his

supply of it and his commitments to buy it in the future are in excess of his commitments to sell it. (See also SHORT.)

LONG-TERM
In corporate life, generally a period in excess of ten years. Long-term planning is planning for the BUSINESS world of ten years hence. Longs, as the British government's long-term bonds used to be called, were securities with an original MATURITY of 15 years or more.

In the long term, we're all dead.
John Maynard Keynes

LOSS
The condition in which a COMPANY's expenses over a given period are greater than its REVENUE over the same period; or where its INCOME from a particular transaction is less than the cost of the transaction.

LOSS ADJUSTER
See ADJUSTER.

LOSS LEADER
A PRODUCT that is sold at a LOSS by a manufacturer or a retailer to entice (that is, to lead) a CUSTOMER to buy other things from the same manufacturer or retailer.

LOYALTY
The extent to which customers buy the same GOODS and SERVICES again and again. On the whole, a CUSTOMER's loyalty decreases as his or her choice gets wider.

LOYALTY CARD
The plastic card issued to customers as part of a LOYALTY PROGRAMME.

LOYALTY PROGRAMME
A MARKETING initiative designed to increase customers' loyalty to a particular PRODUCT or a partic-

ular DISTRIBUTION CHANNEL. A typical loyalty programme might include giving customers plastic cards which electronically credit them with points (which can be redeemed for GOODS) in line with the volume of their purchases.

LTD

A short version of LIMITED LIABILITY, an expression added to the end of a COMPANY's name to indicate that the company has the protection that limited liability affords. All languages have a similar way of indicating that an ORGANISATION enjoys the privileges of limited liability.

LUXURY GOODS

Expensive GOODS which no reasonable person would consider to be essential to everyday life, such as precious jewellery, high fashion or specially matured alcoholic drinks. Because of their nature, luxury goods are bought in a different way from CONSUMER goods and need to be marketed differently. They are sometimes taxed differently, too.

M&A

Short for mergers and acquisitions, the BUSINESS of arranging and financing takeovers (of one corporation by another) and mergers (between corporations).

MACHINE TOOL

A piece of equipment used for cutting and shaping metal in a manufacturing PROCESS.

The factory of the future will have only two employees, a man and a dog. The man will be there to feed the dog, and the dog will be there to keep the man from touching the equipment.

Warren Bennis, American academic

MAIL ORDER

The use of the postal services as a DISTRIBUTION CHANNEL for GOODS. Customers receive a catalogue (a mail-order catalogue) from which they choose goods that they want to buy. They order and pay for them (by telephone or by post) and are sent the goods within a stated time period.

MAILSHOT

A widespread DISTRIBUTION of printed material by post aimed at persuading the recipients to purchase particular GOODS or SERVICES, to join an ORGANISATION, to give MONEY to charity, and so on.

MAINTENANCE

The cost of keeping PLANT and machinery in good working order.

MALL

A shopping environment in which a number of retailers are collected together in a pedestrian-only covered area. Malls have existed in Europe for centuries, but they have been given a new lease of air-conditioned life in the United States.

MANAGE

An age-old word derived from the Italian *man-*

neggiare, to handle (originally horses, now corporations). People who manage (managers) are generally expected to carry out certain functions; for example, employ STAFF, motivate and organise them, plan for the future and innovate (both products and processes).

MANAGED FLOAT
See DIRTY FLOAT.

MANAGEMENT
There are two meanings:

- The BUSINESS of managing an ORGANISATION.
- The people who do the managing.

The basic task of management is to make people productive.
Peter Drucker

MANAGEMENT ACCOUNTS
A set of ACCOUNTS prepared solely for the benefit of the managers of an ORGANISATION. Such accounts need to be non-technical, prepared regularly (every month or every week, for example) and in a consistent format. They often contain forecasts and estimates that break away from the normal constraints of financial facts.

MANAGEMENT BUY-OUT
See MBO.

MANAGEMENT CONSULTANT
A person or ORGANISATION who advises managers in a number of BUSINESS areas, including STRATEGY, INFORMATION TECHNOLOGY, MARKETING and HUMAN RESOURCES. Management consultants analyse business situations and offer advice on how to improve them. Many go on to get involved in implementing their own advice.

MANAGER
See MANAGE.

Managing director
A person who directs the MANAGEMENT of an ORGANISATION; the most senior manager in a BUSINESS, DIVISION or FUNCTION.

Mandate
An instruction to carry out a particular course of action. The instruction may be given by a court, a CUSTOMER, or a manager.

Manufacture
Originally the making of things by hand – "manu"... "facturing" – but now the making of things by hand or by machine.

Margin
In general, the edge. But the word has come to have a number of specialist meanings in BUSINESS:

- The difference between the COST of something and the PRICE at which it is sold, that is, the PROFIT margin.
- In economic theory, the margin is that level of production at which the cost of producing one more unit is exactly equal to the REVENUE to be gained from it.
- A method of trading in securities which involves initially putting up only a small percentage of the cost of the securities, known as margin trading.
- Margin lending is a form of lending by a BANK which enables a CUSTOMER to buy shares and then use the VALUE of the shares as SECURITY for the lending.

Margin call
A demand for extra FUNDS made by a BROKER to an INVESTOR who is involved in MARGIN trading; that is, an investor who is buying securities without paying for them in full.

Marginal cost
The extra cost of producing one more unit of a PRODUCT over and above an agreed output. The

marginal cost assumes that all the overheads have been absorbed by the previous production.

MARGINAL PRODUCER
A manufacturing unit that is only just able to remain profitable at the current PRICE levels of the INDUSTRY in which it is operating, and at its own current production levels. When the economic environment becomes less favourable for the industry, the marginal producer is the first to go out of business.

MARGINAL PROPENSITY
The proportion of any additional unit of INCOME that will be used in a particular way. Thus if a CONSUMER'S marginal propensity to save is 0.3, he or she will save 30 cents out of every extra dollar that they gain.

MARK DOWN
To reduce the original selling PRICE of a PRODUCT, perhaps because it has not been selling well. In particular, to lower the quoted price of a COMPANY'S shares sharply after the announcement of unfavourable news.

MARK UP
The difference between the cost PRICE of a PRODUCT (or service) and its selling price.

MARKET
The place where buyers and sellers come together to exchange GOODS and SERVICES and to determine prices. It is a fundamental concept in ECONOMICS, where buyers represent DEMAND and sellers represent supply. In MARKETING terms, a market refers to a group of consumers with identifiable characteristics in common, such as the teenage market.

Market can also refer to the total sales of a particular PRODUCT or INDUSTRY. For example: "It's a $4 billion market."

MARKET CAPITALISATION
The MARKET VALUE of a COMPANY'S issued shares; that is, the quoted PRICE of each individual SHARE multiplied by the number of shares in ISSUE.

Market leader
The ORGANISATION which has the largest share of any particular MARKET, and whose tactics are watched most closely by the other participants. A market leader's actions set the trend for the rest of the market.

Market penetration
The percentage of a TARGET MARKET that has bought a particular PRODUCT at least once. Also the extent (usually expressed as a percentage) to which a potential market is reached by an ADVERTISING message or a DISTRIBUTION CHANNEL.

Market research
A process of systematically analysing the MARKET for a potential new PRODUCT or service, and/or examining how the market for an existing product or service has changed. Much market research is based on surveys of consumers in which they are asked a series of questions about their purchasing habits. It is sometimes called marketing research.

Market share
The proportion of a MARKET served by one participant. For example: "BMW has an x.y% share of the European car market."

Marketing
The process of identifying, anticipating and satisfying consumers' needs (profitably) by means of the standard tools of marketing, such as MARKET RESEARCH, ADVERTISING and general PROMOTION.

Marketing is the process of taking the guesswork out of hunch.
Anon

Marketing mix
The weight given to various elements involved in MARKETING a product or service. The elements are sometimes classified as the four Ps: PRODUCT, PRICE, place and PROMOTION. In the marketing mix for

LUXURY GOODS, for instance, price is less important than product.

MASS MARKET
A MARKET consisting of almost everybody in the population. The opposite of NICHE MARKET.

MASS PRODUCTION
The production of GOODS (or SERVICES) in large quantities and by a standardised PROCESS with the aim of appealing to a MASS MARKET.

MATERIALS HANDLING
The business of moving the materials involved in a PROCESS (RAW MATERIALS, semi-finished GOODS, or the final PRODUCT) so that they are in the right place at the right time. The COST of materials handling can be as high as 40% of the total cost of manufacturing.

MATERNITY LEAVE
The (usually unpaid) time off work given to a pregnant EMPLOYEE by an EMPLOYER. The employee's job is kept available for her to return to once her baby's dependence has diminished. (See also PATERNITY LEAVE.)

MATRIX ORGANISATION
A COMPANY whose organisational STRUCTURE is designed along two axes, giving each EMPLOYEE two lines of authority. The two axes are most frequently geographic and functional. Hence the head of an American MULTINATIONAL company's German accounting operation will report to both his functional head (the finance director in the United States) and his regional head (the MANAGING DIRECTOR of the business's German subsidiary).

MATURE INDUSTRY
An INDUSTRY in which innovative products and processes are rare and in which the MARKET SHARE of individual firms does not change much over time. Such industries include steelmaking, carmaking and innkeeping.

MATURITY

The length of time left until the PRINCIPAL repayment on a BOND becomes due. The original maturity of the bond is its maturity on the date when it was issued; the residual maturity is its maturity now – that is, the length of time from this moment until the repayment becomes due.

MBA

Short for Master's Degree in Business Administration, the main qualification (rapidly becoming indispensable) for managers and people who want to run their own BUSINESS. The MBA is a postgraduate, post-experience one- or two-year course in which students study STRATEGY, MARKETING, finance and ORGANISATIONAL BEHAVIOUR. MBA courses are particularly popular in the United States; less so in Europe.

MBI

Short for management buy-in (see MBO).

MBO

Short for management buy-out, the purchasing of an ORGANISATION by a group of managers. They may already work for the organisation, or they may be outsiders who intend to work for it once they have purchased it (in which case the deal is sometimes called a management buy-in). An MBO is often also a LEVERAGED BUY-OUT.

MEDIA

The vehicles that carry ADVERTISING (and other things, such as entertainment and news) to an audience. They include television, radio, newspapers, magazines and the INTERNET. Mass media are forms of media that reach a MASS MARKET.

MEDIA BUYER

A person in an ADVERTISING AGENCY or independent FIRM who buys space in the MEDIA in bulk: time during television programmes or pages in newspapers and magazines. Media buyers, sometimes referred to as "gorillas with calculators", then resell the space in smaller quantities to advertisers and advertising agencies.

Mediation
A process of using a THIRD PARTY to resolve a difference of opinion between two other parties. Unlike ARBITRATION, mediation does not involve the conflicting parties agreeing in advance to accept the third party's decision. The mediator has no legal power to enforce an agreement.

Meeting
Any gathering of two or more people in which communication of some sort takes place. In a BUSINESS context, a meeting is more commonly thought of as a formal gathering for the purpose of considering the items on a pre-prepared AGENDA.

Memorandum of association
The formal legal document that lays down the basic details of a COMPANY: its name, its nature (whether it has LIMITED LIABILITY), its registered address and its objectives – that is, the purpose for which it was established.

Mentor
A person assigned to work with a senior manager for the specific purpose of offering independent advice on the manager's performance in the workplace. Mentors must be in a position where they can express contrary views without damaging their career prospects.

Mentoring
The work of a MENTOR. Mentoring is partly designed to overcome the oft-repeated claim that it is lonely at the top.

Menu
The list of options that appear on a computer screen when a user asks to start a new PROGRAM.

Merchandise
GOODS and SERVICES in a finished state, ready to go

to the retailer or already in the hands of the retailer.

MERCHANT BANK
The traditional British term for INVESTMENT BANK. Many merchant banks (most of them based in the City of London) grew out of the families (the Rothschilds, Hambros and Barings, for instance) who financed the TRADE of Britain's merchants during the years of the British empire. Hence the name.

MERGER
The amicable coming together of two companies into one.

MERGER ACCOUNTING
A particular method of taking mergers into account – that is, of putting together the separate ACCOUNTS of two merged companies. Merger accounting avoids creating GOODWILL. It includes assets in the combined accounts at their existing book values rather than at the price that was actually paid for them. (That method requires goodwill as a device to fill the gap between book value and price.)

MERGERS AND ACQUISITIONS
See M&A.

MEZZANINE FINANCE
Any type of finance that falls somewhere between EQUITY and DEBT in the priority of its claim in the case of a LIQUIDATION. If equity is the first floor and debt the ground floor, the mezzanine stands somewhere in between.

MFN
Short for most favoured nation, a status granted by one country to another whereby the first country agrees to apply its lowest tariffs to the second country's EXPORTS. This means that no other country's exports will get better treatment.

Middle manager
A manager who sits somewhere in the middle of an ORGANISATION's hierarchy; a general term for the great bulk of managers who are neither managing directors nor new graduate recruits. Many middle managers have been dispensed with as a result of DELAYERING.

Mineral rights
The right to dig for the minerals that lie under a particular piece of ground.

The meek shall inherit the earth, but not the mineral rights.
J. Paul Getty

Minimum wage
The lowest amount that can legally be paid to an EMPLOYEE, often expressed as an hourly sum.

Minority
A SHAREHOLDER (or group of shareholders) who owns less than 50% of a COMPANY. In some situations, such as a TAKEOVER, the interests of minorities are protected by law.

Minutes
The written record of a MEETING. Companies retain the minutes of important meetings, such as BOARD meetings, as a formal acknowledgement and reminder of decisions that have been reached.

Mission
A COMPANY's overriding BUSINESS purpose; something that it aims to do above and beyond making a PROFIT.

Mission statement
A written version of a COMPANY's MISSION, which aims to inspire its WORKFORCE and, by giving them the feeling that they are working for a higher purpose than wages, to make them more productive and more loyal.

MOBILITY
See LABOUR MOBILITY.

MODEM
An abbreviation of modulator-demodulator, the instrument which sits between a computer and a telephone line and allows electronic messages to be passed in and out of the former via the latter. Without modems there would be no public access to the INTERNET.

MONEY
Anything that is recognised as a store of VALUE and a medium of exchange by the participants in a MARKET. This could be (and has been) cowrie shells, black beads and dollar bills.

A business that makes nothing but money is a poor sort of business.
Henry Ford

MONEY MARKET
A MARKET in which financial institutions (such as banks) buy and sell SHORT-TERM financial instruments among themselves.

MONEY SUPPLY
The amount of MONEY circulating in an economy. The definition of money varies. In the M0 version it consists of notes and coins only. The M1, M2 and M3 versions include a varying range of SHORT-TERM financial assets (such as BANK deposits) as well as notes and coins.

A monopoly is a terrible thing until you've got one.
Rupert Murdoch

MONOPOLY
The situation where a single producer has a sufficiently large SHARE of a MARKET to be able to control prices in that market. A monopoly implies the

absence of COMPETITION. Governments and CONSUMER watchdogs aim to prevent companies with a monopoly from abusing their dominant position at the expense of the consumer.

MONOPSONY
The situation where a single CUSTOMER has the whole of a market to itself; the mirror image of a MONOPOLY. Monopsonies occur most frequently when a government is virtually the only customer for a particular product, for example, in the defence INDUSTRY or in certain areas of medical care.

MOODY'S
One of the world's three main CREDIT-RATING agencies. Moody's judgment on the quality of a COMPANY or a country's DEBT can materially affect the PRICE that the company or country has to pay to borrow MONEY.

It's a good thing to make mistakes … so long as you're found out quickly.
John Maynard Keynes

MOONLIGHTING
The earning of a second INCOME; for example, night-time taxi driving by someone who is a builder or a civil servant by day. Moonlighting is so called because it frequently (but not necessarily) takes place at night. It also implies that the work is not 100% legal, in particular that it is kept out of sight of the taxman.

MORATORIUM
A period of time in which a borrower is allowed (with the approval of the lender) to forgo payments of PRINCIPAL on a LOAN. Financial institutions are rarely prepared to grant borrowers a moratorium on INTEREST payments.

MORTGAGE
A LONG-TERM LOAN for the purposes of buying REAL ESTATE which uses the real estate as SECURITY for the loan.

Motion
A formal proposition made in a MEETING which seeks to gain the support of those at the meeting for a particular course of action. Properly formulated motions are automatically recorded in the MINUTES of the meeting.

Mouse
The small attachment to a computer that allows the user to go in and out of different SOFTWARE programs. The mouse controls the movements of a cursor on the screen. By clicking the mouse when the cursor points to a particular ICON, the user can switch from one PROGRAM to another.

Multimedia
The use of a number of different MEDIA simultaneously. For example, a multimedia presentation might include a video film (using a television), some sound effects on a CD, a slide show, and a number of graphic posters.

Multinational
A COMPANY which has production and sales operations in a number of countries, and which co-ordinates these operations from a single HEADQUARTERS. The operations are run separately from each other, unlike those of a TRANSNATIONAL.

Mutual
A mutual ORGANISATION is one that is run for the benefit of a group of people (its members) who have set it up to provide GOODS or SERVICES for themselves. Savings banks and INSURANCE companies were frequently set up in this way in the 19th century. In general, the members of a mutual organisation also own it.

NAFTA
The ACRONYM for North American Free Trade Agreement, an agreement between Canada, the United States and Mexico that aims to remove tariffs and other barriers to TRADE between the three countries.

NATIONALISE
A privately owned corporation is nationalised when it is purchased (often compulsorily) by the state. Companies are usually nationalised for a principle (for example, a belief that the defence INDUSTRY should be controlled by the state for reasons of security) rather than for PROFIT. Nationalised companies are rarely as profitable as privately owned ones. (See also PRIVATISATION.)

NEGOTIABLE INSTRUMENT
A financial instrument, such as a BEARER BOND or a SHARE, which can be transferred from one owner to another without informing the original issuer of the instrument.

NEGOTIATION
The process of reaching agreement between two parties, one of which has something that the other party wants, and for which the other party is prepared to give something in return.

NEPOTISM
The granting of favours to members of the same family, an issue central to the running of a FAMILY FIRM. How can it remain a family firm without undermining the morale of non-family employees by its nepotism?

NET
A VALUE that is left after certain deductions have been made from a GROSS amount.

NET ASSET BACKING
The NET WORTH of a COMPANY divided by the number of its shares; a rough approximation of the VALUE behind each SHARE.

NET PRESENT VALUE

The VALUE today of an amount that is to be paid in the future. This value is calculated by taking into account future INTEREST rates and the risk that the payment will not eventually be made. Net present value is frequently used to judge the viability of an INVESTMENT project. If the net present value of its expected REVENUE exceeds the net present value of its future costs then it is worth going ahead.

NET PROFIT

An ORGANISATION'S GROSS INCOME less all its costs, including TAX, DEPRECIATION and INTEREST payments.

NET WORTH

An ORGANISATION'S assets less its liabilities. The amount that would be left to shareholders were all the organisation's assets to be sold and all its liabilities to be met at the values that the accountants have ascribed to them.

NETWORK

The links that exist between computers enabling users of them to share certain centralised data and/or services, and to communicate among themselves.

Banks and securities firms risk being reduced to a line or two of application code on a network.

John Reed, when chairman of Citicorp

NETWORKING

Making contact with other people in the hope that they might subsequently be useful in BUSINESS or elsewhere. The expression has grown out of the computer INDUSTRY'S use of the word NETWORK.

NEW ENTRANT

A COMPANY that enters a MARKET for the first time. New entrants inevitably provoke a strategic response from existing companies within the market.

Newsletter
A publication that specialises in breaking news in a narrow area; for example, a country, an INDUSTRY or a MARKET.

Niche market
A small, narrowly defined MARKET, such as the market for Rolls-Royce motor cars, or the market for newsletters about biotechnology. Small, innovative companies are particularly good at identifying and satisfying niche markets.

Your company does not belong in any market where it can't be the best.
Philip Kotler

Nikkei-Dow Jones average
A leading share INDEX of the Tokyo STOCK EXCHANGE. It is an average of 225 major stocks of the Tokyo market.

Nominal
A nominal amount may be one that is too small to mention (as in nominal DAMAGES) or one that exists only in name (as in the nominal PRICE of potatoes in 1945, a price that is not adjusted for the ravages of INFLATION, which the so-called REAL price is). The nominal VALUE of a SHARE is the value on the SHARE CERTIFICATE, which may not be a price that anybody has ever actually paid for it.

Nominee
A person whose name is used in place of somebody else's. A nominee may open a Swiss BANK ACCOUNT, for instance, to disguise the identity of the real beneficiary of the account.

Non-executive director
Any DIRECTOR on the BOARD of a COMPANY who is not also an EXECUTIVE working for the company. A non-executive director's role is to ensure that there is a healthy balance between the interests of

shareholders and the interests of the company's MANAGEMENT.

Pet rocks.

Ross Perot when referring to the non-executive directors of General Motors

NON-PERFORMING

A LOAN on which INTEREST has not been paid for a considerable period of time (usually three months) is said to be non-performing. Financial institutions have to treat such loans in a special way in their ACCOUNTS, setting aside RESERVES against the possibility that they will never get their MONEY back.

NON-REFUNDABLE

Any advance payment for a PRODUCT or service that will not be repaid if the product or service is ultimately not wanted by the payer. For instance, a deposit to secure a house which is not yet built may be non-refundable should the purchase not be completed.

NON-TARIFF BARRIER

A barrier to TRADE other than a TARIFF imposed directly on an import at its point of entry. Non-tariff barriers include things like safety regulations which only domestic firms satisfy; DISTRIBUTION systems that discriminate against IMPORTS; and government regulations that demand SERVICES (like finance) be supplied by known individuals.

NON-VOTING SHARE

A SHARE in a COMPANY that does not give the holder the right to vote at company meetings. Holders of non-voting shares benefit financially in the same way as other shareholders, but they have no say in the running of the company whose shares they own. In some markets the issuing of such shares is frowned upon.

NOT-FOR-PROFIT ORGANISATION
An American expression for organisations which have other reasons for existing apart from the maximisation of PROFIT. They include charities, foundations and educational institutions. The TAX treatment of such organisations is often different from that of a for-profit corporation.

NOTE
A written acknowledgement of a DEBT, as in pound note or PROMISSORY NOTE.

NOTEBOOK COMPUTER
A miniature LAPTOP COMPUTER with a more limited range of SOFTWARE.

NOTICE
Advice given in advance. The advice may be of a forthcoming MEETING, or of a person's wish to end a period of employment. For example: "Today he handed in his notice."

NUMBERED ACCOUNT
A BANK ACCOUNT that is known to most of the bank's STAFF only by its number. No name appears on the account's cheques or on the statements. The main purpose of the numbered account is to disguise the identity of the account holder. Most countries (including Switzerland) insist nowadays that the true beneficiary of all accounts be known to at least one senior manager in the bank.

O&M
Short for organisation and methods, a once-popular field of MANAGEMENT study dedicated to improving the methods and procedures used in OFFICE environments.

OBJECTIVE
The ultimate goal of an ORGANISATION'S STRATEGY.

Aim for the highest.
Andrew Carnegie

OBSOLESCENCE
The capacity of something to become out-of-date. For example, all fashion garments have a built-in obsolescence, that is, by their very nature they need to be replaced next season.

OCCUPANCY
A measure of the extent to which a property is occupied. For example, an apartment that is rented for only half the year has a 50% occupancy; a hotel room that is occupied for nine nights out of every ten has a 90% occupancy.

OCCUPATION
The paid employment that occupies most of an individual's working life.

OCCUPATIONAL HAZARD
A danger that arises as a result of a person's OCCUPATION. Hence falling off ladders is an occupational hazard for window-cleaners; backache is an occupational hazard of computer programmers.

OCCUPATIONAL PENSION
A PENSION that is paid by a person's EMPLOYER by dint of the years of employment and the contributions that were made to the employer's PENSION FUND during that period.

OECD
Short for Organisation for Economic Co-operation

and Development, a Paris-based ORGANISATION of 29 (richish) nations. Among other things, the OECD aims to harmonise international trading practices and to promote FREE TRADE.

OFF BALANCE SHEET
Any transaction by a COMPANY that does not appear on its BALANCE SHEET. Off-balance-sheet items include things like LEASING deals and FIDUCIARY deposits.

OFF-THE-SHELF
Something that is purchased straight off a shop's shelf, a PRODUCT produced in advance in the expectation that it will find a CONSUMER who is prepared to buy it. The opposite of tailor-made or CUSTOMISED.

An off-the-shelf COMPANY is one that is bought with its legal status already established, that is, a company that has never carried out BUSINESS but which has a name, ARTICLES OF ASSOCIATION and a registered address.

OFFER
An indication of willingness to enter into an agreement, and of the terms of such an agreement. An offer and an acceptance constitute a legally binding CONTRACT.

OFFICE
There are two meanings:

- A room containing a desk and a chair in which people work on paper or on computers.
- A clearly defined role within an ORGANISATION. For example, something that has to be done by the CHAIRMAN's office is done by whoever happens to be carrying out the function of chairman.

OFFICE POLITICS
The art of organising a group of people who work in offices. More specifically, the expression refers

to the psychological games that people play with each other in and out of the OFFICE.

OFFSHORE
In general, any BUSINESS that is transacted in foreign currencies between parties that are also foreign to the place. A Dutch BANK based in London lending dollars to a Brazilian COMPANY is transacting offshore business. Such business is often done in order to minimise tax liabilities. (See TAX HAVEN.)

OLIGOPOLY
The control of a MARKET by a few producers. The danger of an oligopoly is that the few producers get together and agree among themselves to fix prices as if they were a MONOPOLY.

OMBUDSMAN
An independent person appointed to hear and act upon consumers' complaints about manufacturers or service providers. The idea originated in Sweden, where the first ombudsman was set up to hear complaints about government services.

ON APPROVAL
When GOODS are supplied on the understanding that the purchaser may return them if they prove not to be what the purchaser wanted. Goods bought by MAIL ORDER are usually, in effect, sold on approval.

ON-LINE
A computer that is linked directly to a DATABASE or to a central processing unit.

ON SPEC
Work done for a client without a CONTRACT or ORDER on the understanding that the client will only pay for the work if and when it is used.

OPEN-MARKET OPERATIONS
Dealings by a CENTRAL BANK in the MONEY MARKET designed to adjust a country's MONEY SUPPLY.

OPEN POSITION
A situation in which an INVESTOR has an obligation to buy more securities of a certain type in the future than his future obligation to sell securities of that type. (Or the other way round, he has an obligation to sell more than he has to buy.)

OPEN PLAN
A way of designing the interior of an OFFICE in which the walls dividing the space into individual rooms are removed. All that may stand between employees' desks are potted plants and soundproof screening,

OPEN OUTCRY
A method of trading on an exchange in which dealers shout out their offers to buy or sell. A CONTRACT is made when a buyer's shouts are matched with those of a seller.

OPEN SYSTEM
An expression used to describe INFORMATION TECHNOLOGY that is accessible to all. In other words, any HARDWARE and SOFTWARE that are in the public domain so that manufacturers can make products that are compatible with them.

OPERATING PROFIT
The difference between those revenues and costs which are directly related to an ORGANISATION'S main lines of BUSINESS. Operating PROFIT thus excludes any extraordinary INCOME or expenditure and the COST of finance.

OPERATING SYSTEM
The fundamental software PROGRAM that enables a computer to run all the other programs that it contains.

OPERATIONS RESEARCH
A mathematically based study of repetitive activity designed to improve the productivity of manufacturing processes. OR, as it is known, makes considerable use of computerised simulation.

Opportunity cost
In general, the amount that could have been gained if FACTORS OF PRODUCTION (land, LABOUR or CAPITAL) had been put to an alternative (and more rewarding) use. Hence investing in a BANK ACCOUNT earning 3% a year when the STOCKMARKET INDEX rises by 10% has an opportunity cost of 7%.

Option
The right to buy or sell a specified amount of a COMMODITY (or of securities) at a specified PRICE within a specified time (usually less than six months). Such a right can be bought and sold during the specified time. If it is not exercised within that time, however, it expires.

Order
An instruction to buy or sell GOODS or SERVICES which is legally binding.

Order form
The document on which an ORDER is formally recorded.

Ordinary share
The most straightforward form of SHARE. It gives the holder the right to vote at formal shareholders' meetings, and the right to a portion of any dividends that are declared, but nothing more. (See also PREFERENCE SHARE.)

Organic growth
The growth of an ORGANISATION that comes from its own internal efforts rather than from external factors, such as a TAKEOVER or a JOINT VENTURE.

Organisations exist to enable ordinary people to do extraordinary things.
Ted Levitt, professor of marketing at Harvard

Organisation
There are two BUSINESS-related meanings:

- A collection of people who come together for a defined purpose.
- The way in which those people structure their relationships to best achieve their purpose.

ORGANISATIONAL BEHAVIOUR
The academic study of the behaviour of people within organisations. It embraces subjects like motivation and LEADERSHIP.

ORGANOGRAM
A diagrammatic representation of an ORGANISATION'S STRUCTURE, including lines representing the relationships between different functions and different businesses.

ORIGINAL MATURITY
See MATURITY.

OTC
See OVER-THE-COUNTER.

OUTPLACEMENT
Assistance given to dismissed employees by their former EMPLOYER to help them to find a new job or career. The function is increasingly carried out by specialist outplacement agencies.

OUTSOURCE
To hand over to an outside ORGANISATION the responsibility for running and developing a discrete FUNCTION or PROCESS within a BUSINESS. For example, an organisation might outsource the running of its computers or its fleet of company cars.

OUTSTANDING
An obligation that is due and that has not yet been settled.

OUTWORKER
Someone who works for an ORGANISATION somewhere outside the organisation's own PREMISES. Outworkers are used, for example, in the textiles

INDUSTRY, where they assemble garments in their own homes. They are usually paid a PIECE RATE which relates their rewards to the quantity of GOODS that they produce.

OVERCHARGE

To demand a PRICE for something that is in excess of the price that can be obtained elsewhere, all other things being equal.

OVERDRAFT

A CREDIT FACILITY granted by a BANK which allows the borrower to draw FUNDS from the bank up to a prescribed limit, as and when the borrower wishes. This flexible form of borrowing is common in Europe but not widespread in North America or East Asia.

Remember that credit is money.

Benjamin Franklin

OVERHEAD

A COMPANY'S overhead is the sum of its DIRECT COSTS.

OVERSUBSCRIBE

When the DEMAND for a new ISSUE of securities exceeds the supply of securities available, the issue is said to be oversubscribed. If there is a demand for 700,000 securities and there are only 100,000 for SALE, the issue is said to be six times oversubscribed.

OVER-THE-COUNTER

There are two meanings:

- An informal STOCKMARKET for trading in shares that are not quoted on a major exchange, known as an OTC MARKET.
- Pharmaceuticals that can be sold freely over a shop's counter without the need for a doctor's prescription.

Overtime

Hours worked by an EMPLOYEE beyond those contractually agreed with the EMPLOYER; for example, work done in the evenings or at weekends. Overtime is usually paid at a higher rate than work done in normal hours.

The highest reward for a man's toil is not what he gets for it, but what he becomes.

John Ruskin

Overtrading

Increasing a BUSINESS's TURNOVER to such an extent and at such a speed that the increase is not supported by other areas of the business. If the ACCOUNTS department is swamped with new orders, for example, and cannot get invoices out and payments in within a reasonable time, the business might suffer from a LIQUIDITY crisis.

Own label

Products that are branded with the name of the retailer, such as a supermarket which sells its own-label cornflakes and soap powder in COMPETITION with established manufacturers' products. The retailer itself does not actually MANUFACTURE cornflakes or soap powder. It does not even manufacture the packaging. It just adds its name to products that have been made by someone else, sometimes someone who produces a well-known competing BRAND.

Owner-operator

Someone who owns and runs their own small BUSINESS – a taxi-driver or someone who runs a corner shop.

P&L
See PROFIT AND LOSS ACCOUNT.

PACIFIC RIM
Any grouping of countries which have coastlines on the Pacific Ocean.

PACKING LIST
A formal list of the contents of a container which is sent with the container. The person who receives the container checks that its contents accord with the packing list to see if anything has gone missing in transit.

PAID-UP CAPITAL
That part of a COMPANY'S AUTHORISED CAPITAL which has been fully paid for by the company's shareholders.

PALLET
A wooden frame on which GOODS are placed when in transit. A pallet is designed to reduce damage to the goods and to make them easier to handle.

PAPER OFFER
An offer by one COMPANY to buy another in exchange not for CASH but for shares in the purchasing company (that is, its paper). The vendor thus merely exchanges the shares of one company for those of another.

PAPER PROFIT
An unrealised PROFIT which only appears on paper, that is, as a calculation. For instance, if shares bought for $300 are now worth $500, but their owner has no intention of selling them, the owner can be said to have made a paper profit of $200.

PAR
The NOMINAL (or face) VALUE of a SECURITY. The PRICE written on the certificate that provides proof of ownership.

Parallel market
A MARKET that operates outside the standard market for a PRODUCT or service; for example, European shares that are sold as ADRS in the United States; or the street vendor who sells GOODS outside a store which also sells the same goods, but at a different PRICE.

Parameter
A constant that helps to set a framework for considering issues that are variable. For example, a COMPANY'S parameters for determining its STRATEGY for the next year could be that the rate of growth of the economy will be 3% and that it wants to increase its MARKET SHARE by 10%.

Parent company
A COMPANY which owns one or more subsidiaries.

Parkinson's Law
First expounded in 1958 in a book written by a history professor, Cyril Northcote Parkinson, the law says that "work expands to fill the time available for its completion". Another allied law says that expenditure rises to meet INCOME.

Partly paid
Shares for which a SHAREHOLDER has paid only part of the amount that is due. The rest of the payment can usually be called for at the issuer's discretion.

The partner of my partner is not my partner.
Lawyers' maxim

Partnership
Two or more people who get together to undertake a BUSINESS for PROFIT, but without becoming incorporated as a COMPANY. This is a common form of ORGANISATION among professional people such as lawyers and accountants. In some countries partnerships have a separate legal existence; in others there is no legal existence separate from that of the individual partners themselves. (See

also LIMITED PARTNERSHIP.)

PART SHIPMENT
The shipping of one part of a larger ORDER or consignment of GOODS. Part shipments can create problems if the documentation is not handled properly.

PART-TIME WORK
Any work that takes up less than a normal full working day. Part-time workers are rarely entitled to the same PENSION and health benefits as full-time workers.

PASSIVE INVESTOR
An INVESTOR in a START-UP COMPANY who is looking only for financial gain. A passive investor has no interest in being involved in the running and building of the BUSINESS.

PASSWORD
A closely guarded sequence of alphanumeric characters which have to be entered into a computer before gaining access to it and its SOFTWARE programs. The password acts as a security device.

PATENT
A document given to an inventor by a registered authority granting the inventor the exclusive rights to MANUFACTURE and sell his invention in a specified MARKET for a specified period of time. When that time is over, the PRODUCT is said to come off patent.

PATENT PENDING
Notification, often written on the side of a PRODUCT, to say that a PATENT for the product has been applied for, but has not yet been granted.

PATERNITY LEAVE
Time that a male EMPLOYEE is allowed off work to help his partner with a new-born child. During paternity leave the father's job remains open to

him, awaiting his return. (See also MATERNITY LEAVE.)

Pay
The reward for LABOUR.

Payback period
The amount of time that it takes for an INVESTMENT to pay for itself; that is, the time until the discounted INCOME from the investment exactly equals the CAPITAL put into the investment.

Payday
The day on which employees receive their pay.

Don't be afraid to make a mistake. But be sure you don't make the same mistake twice.
Akio Morita, founder of Sony

PAYE
The ACRONYM for pay as you earn, a way of collecting INCOME TAX at source, that is, from full-time employees as and when they are paid.

Payment date
The date on which an acknowledged payment is due; for example, dividends that have been declared but not yet paid, or an INVOICE for work done that is due to be paid a fixed number of days after the work has been completed.

Payment method
The means by which a due payment is made, that is, by CASH, CHEQUE, CREDIT CARD, BANK DRAFT, or whatever.

Payroll
The list of all the employees within an ORGANISATION that are paid on a regular basis. Also the aggregate total of all that is paid to those employees on a regular basis.

PC
Short for personal computer, a stand-alone computer CUSTOMISED for each individual user. The PC marked a revolution from earlier generations of computers which had been large centralised machines operated by specialists.

P/E RATIO
Short for price/earnings ratio, the ratio of a SHARE'S STOCKMARKET PRICE to its EARNINGS PER SHARE. The ratio is seen as a key indicator of whether a company is over-valued or not. Each INDUSTRY has a P/E ratio that is considered more or less average for that industry.

PENSION
An INCOME that is paid after someone's retirement from work because of contributions that were made to a FUND during their working life. Pension contributions are a standard PERK offered by companies to attract and retain good employees.

PENSION FUND
A FUND set up to meet the PENSION obligations of an ORGANISATION. In many countries pension funds are among the largest investors in the STOCKMARKET.

PEPPERCORN RENT
An extremely low NOMINAL RENT paid for BUSINESS PREMISES, often because the premises are due to be redeveloped at some uncertain future date and may have to be vacated at short notice.

PER DIEM
A daily allowance given to an EMPLOYEE to cover expenses, for things like travel and entertainment, incurred in the course of their work.

PERFORMANCE BOND
A written commitment to perform a piece of work to a specified standard and within a specified period of time. Failure to meet the criteria of the bond can lead to the payment of heavy penalties.

Performance bonds are common in the construction business.

Performance-related pay
Relating a significant proportion of an EMPLOYEE's pay to their performance. The concept is hard to put into practice because of the difficulty in finding a quantifiable measure that is genuinely related to an individual's performance. The most obvious candidates, SHARE PRICE and PROFIT, have obvious shortcomings.

Perishable goods
GOODS which perish fairly quickly, such as fresh fish, fruit or dairy products.

Perk
Short for perquisite, an incidental BENEFIT that accrues to an EMPLOYEE because of his or her employment. For example, someone who works in a restaurant might expect free meals to be one of the perks of the job.

Personnel
Traditionally, the department in an ORGANISATION which looks after the day-to-day requirements of its employees. Nowadays it is likely to have been rebranded as HUMAN RESOURCES.

The Peter Principle
A rule first enunciated in a 1969 book by Laurence J. Peter. The Peter Principle says that every EMPLOYEE eventually rises to their level of incompetence. Also expressed as "cream rises until it sours".

Petty cash
Small amounts of CASH retained in the workplace for making occasional small payments in CASH – for milk, stamps, and so on.

Picket
An EMPLOYEE who stands at the entrance to his or her place of work during an industrial dispute in

order to persuade other employees (and/or suppliers and/or customers) not to enter. In many countries where picketing is legal, secondary picketing (the picketing of somebody else's place of work) is not.

Pie chart

A widely used diagrammatic way of presenting business statistics. A pie is drawn to represent the whole of, say, a MARKET or BUSINESS, and the pie is then divided into slices whose size is proportional to the share of the whole that each one represents.

Piece rate

A method of payment for work based on the quantity produced, in contrast to the more common method of payment which is based on the number of hours worked.

Piece work

Work that is performed by outsiders who are paid on a PIECE RATE basis; common in the garment INDUSTRY.

Pilot

A trial run on a modest scale to test the feasibility of something much bigger. For example, the MANUFACTURE of a small number of items of a PRODUCT to see whether it is worth gearing up for their MASS PRODUCTION.

PIN

The ACRONYM for personal identification number, the number required by individuals to gain access to electronic information that is personal and private to them. PINS are most commonly used in association with plastic credit cards.

Pitch

There are two BUSINESS-related meanings:

- To make a prepared presentation with the aim of securing a CONTRACT or SALE.

- The physical space where a street trader (or a STOCKBROKER who operates on the floor of an exchange) has their stall.

PLACEMENT
A method of selling securities in which the securities are placed with a small number of investors. A placement is usually done privately, in contrast to the other main way of selling shares (which is through a public offering). A placement is cheaper than a public offering, but the PRICE obtained for the securities may be less.

Plans are nothing; planning is everything.
President Dwight D. Eisenhower

PLANNING
The formal process of planning for the future of a BUSINESS. Traditionally, this occurs at regular intervals and involves managers outlining a series of actions for the business over, say, the next ten years. (See also BUSINESS PLAN.)

The seeds of every company's demise are contained in its business plan.
Fred Adler, American businessman

PLANT AND EQUIPMENT
A collective term for the tools and machines required to carry on a BUSINESS; everything apart from the buildings and the WORKFORCE.

POINT OF SALE
The place where a SALE is made. This is usually a shop, but it can be a telephone or an ORDER form in a MAIL-ORDER catalogue.

POISON PILL
A tactic followed by a COMPANY to make itself less attractive to a potential buyer. It might include an agreement to distribute large sums of money to shareholders and employees, a DISTRIBUTION that is

triggered only by the appearance of a TAKEOVER BID.

POPULATION
A MARKETING expression for the whole of a potential MARKET for a particular PRODUCT or service.

PORTFOLIO
A mixture of assets (usually financial) that belong to a single owner, either an individual or an institution. A portfolio might typically contain shares, bonds, gold and CASH.

PORTFOLIO MANAGER
The person who looks after an INVESTOR'S PORTFOLIO, buying and selling financial assets (on behalf of the investor) in search of a chosen INVESTMENT target.

PORTFOLIO WORK
A form of work in which an individual has a number of regular jobs which he or she performs at various times throughout the working week.

PORTABLE PENSION
A PENSION that is a PERK of one particular job and which the beneficiary can take with them (and continue to fund) as and when they change jobs.

POSITION
There are several BUSINESS-related meanings:

- A particular job in an ORGANISATION (as in, she has a senior position at *The Economist*).
- An INVESTOR'S STAKE in a particular financial MARKET (including what it owns and what it is contractually obliged to buy and sell in the future).
- The strategic location in a market taken (or aimed for) by a COMPANY.

POST-DATE
To put a future date on a financial instrument (such as a CHEQUE) so that the payee cannot obtain payment until that date.

PPP
See PURCHASING POWER PARITY.

PREDATORY PRICING
The practice of cutting drastically and deliberately the PRICE of a PRODUCT or service in order to steal a COMPETITOR'S MARKET SHARE. By implication, predatory pricing involves cutting prices so that the PROFIT MARGIN is zero or negative. Hence it can only be done as a SHORT-TERM measure.

PRE-EMPTION
The right to purchase something before others can. It refers, in particular, to the right of existing shareholders in a COMPANY to purchase any new ISSUE of shares in the company before the shares are offered to others.

PREFERENCE
Special treatment given by one country to another in respect of TRADE between them. (See also GSP.)

PREFERENCE SHARE
A special sort of SHARE whose DIVIDEND payment has preference over the dividend payments to the holders of ordinary shares. In the event of a LIQUIDATION, owners of preference shares receive payment before ordinary shareholders.

PREFERENTIAL CREDITOR
A CREDITOR of an ORGANISATION who gets priority in certain circumstances, such as a LIQUIDATION. Preferential creditors include TAX authorities, anyone with a CHARGE on the organisation's assets, and lowly paid employees whose wages are overdue.

PREFERRED SUPPLIER
A SUPPLIER who has a special relationship with a CUSTOMER. This relationship usually means that the customer will, other things being equal, give the supplier a certain amount of (almost guaranteed) BUSINESS during the course of a year. In return, the supplier is expected to match certain standards of quality and timeliness.

Premises
The land and buildings where a BUSINESS is carried on.

Premium
There are two BUSINESS-related meanings:

- A regular payment to an insurer for providing COVER against a stated RISK.
- An amount paid over and above some specified VALUE. In the TAKEOVER of a PUBLIC COMPANY, for instance, the premium is the amount paid over and above the PRICE of the company's shares on the STOCKMARKET before the BID appeared.

Prepayment
The settlement of a DEBT before it becomes due. Some LOAN contracts impose a penalty fee if a borrower makes a prepayment.

He who fails to prepare must prepare to fail.
Anon

Presentation
The formal delivery of a BUSINESS message.

Price
The COST in MONEY terms of a PRODUCT or service.

A man who knows the price of everything and the value of nothing.
Oscar Wilde's definition of a cynic

Price sensitive
A PRODUCT or service whose sales fluctuate dramatically with any change in its PRICE. COMMODITY products in markets where there is plenty of COMPETITION are particularly price sensitive. A retailer cannot change the PRICE of a basic loaf of bread, for example, without sharply affecting sales.

Price support
A minimum PRICE set by a government for a PRODUCT in order to guarantee that its producers will obtain a certain INCOME for their output. It is usually applied to agricultural products.

Price war
A fierce form of COMPETITION in which vendors successively undercut each others' prices to steal MARKET SHARE.

When buyers don't fall for prices,
prices must fall for buyers.
Anon

Primary market
The MARKET in which financial instruments are sold when they are first issued, that is, when they pass from the issuer to their first purchaser. Thereafter they are bought and sold in a SECONDARY MARKET.

Prime rate
The INTEREST RATE which banks charge on loans to their most favoured customers.

Prime time
The time when the largest audience is watching commercial television or listening to commercial radio. Advertisers pay the highest rates to have their advertisements broadcast during prime time.

Principal
The amount borrowed in a LOAN or ISSUE of securities. The principal is the CAPITAL sum that has ultimately to be repaid, and on which the INTEREST that has to be paid in the meantime is calculated.

Private company
A COMPANY whose shares are not available to be bought by the general public. A private company is owned by a small number of shareholders who have no obligations (outside the general laws of the land) to reveal information about their BUSINESS

to the public.

Privatisation
The SALE of a state-owned COMPANY to the general public.

Pro forma
A presentation of financial or accounting figures based on a theoretical future occurrence. For instance, a pro-forma set of ACCOUNTS might be produced to show what would happen to their accounts if two companies were to merge. A pro-forma INVOICE indicates the LIABILITY that will arise if an ORDER is made or if certain GOODS are shipped. In practice, pro-forma invoices are often issued simply because CUSTOMS AND EXCISE require that they are. The amount on the invoice may bear little relation to what the CUSTOMER is actually going to pay for the goods.

Process
A number of activities which, taken together, add VALUE to a BUSINESS. This can be as wide as something like MARKETING (the marketing process) or as narrow as a small part of manufacturing (the paint-handling process).

Procurement
The purchasing of all the inputs that are required to keep a BUSINESS running, including RAW MATERIALS, spare parts and machines.

Product
The final output of a manufacturing PROCESS.

Product liability
The LIABILITY of a manufacturer for any PRODUCT which it puts on to the MARKET and that subsequently causes damage to a CONSUMER. In developed countries this liability is becoming embedded in law and not dependent on the CONSUMER proving that the manufacturer was negligent.

PRODUCT LINE
See ASSEMBLY LINE.

PRODUCTIVITY
An economist's term for the output produced in a given time by a unit of any of the three FACTORS OF PRODUCTION (land, LABOUR or CAPITAL). For example, the RETURN produced by an INVESTMENT of $1,000 in a year, or the yield in a year from planting wheat on a hectare of land. Its numerical precision makes productivity a useful way of measuring differences in efficiency over time, or the difference between alternative uses of the factors of production.

PRODUCT RECALL
See RECALL.

PROFIT
What is left over in a BUSINESS after all its bills have been paid. The difference between the REVENUE of the business (from selling its output) and the COST of the inputs that were required to produce the output.

PROFIT AND LOSS ACCOUNT
The ACCOUNTANT'S record of a BUSINESS'S REVENUE and expenditure during a period. Designed to show the PROFIT (or LOSS) that the business made in that period, it is known in the United States as the INCOME STATEMENT.

PROFIT CENTRE
A BUSINESS unit that prepares its own PROFIT AND LOSS ACCOUNT, recording the theoretical prices at which it buys inputs from other parts of the business, and the theoretical prices at which it sells its output to other parts of the business.

PROFIT MARGIN
See MARGIN.

PROFIT SHARING
A way of allowing employees to share in the PROFIT of the ORGANISATION for which they work.

Devising profit-sharing schemes in such a way that everyone feels they are fair has proved to be extremely difficult.

PROFITABILITY

The ability of a particular BUSINESS, PRODUCT or PROCESS to make a PROFIT. There is no single satisfactory measure of a COMPANY's profitability. Proxies include the gross profit MARGIN, the EARNINGS PER SHARE and the RETURN on total assets.

PROGRAM

A set of instructions which enable a computer to carry out particular actions. A word-processing program, for example, enables its user to type letters and data.

Progress might have been all right once,
but it's gone on too long.
Ogden Nash, American humorist

PROJECT FINANCE

A way of financing big CAPITAL projects, such as hydroelectric schemes or toll roads, that depends primarily on the future CASH FLOW of the project for its RETURN.

PROMISSORY NOTE

A legally binding promise by one party to another that a certain payment will be made on a prescribed date in the future. Often referred to simply as a NOTE.

Always be nice to people on the way up because
you'll meet the same people on the way down.
Anon

PROMOTION

There are two BUSINESS-related meanings:

- The elevation of an EMPLOYEE to a more senior POSITION.

- The concentration of exceptional MARKETING effort on a particular PRODUCT or service.

PROPRIETARY
A right that endures for some time for a special reason; for example, a right to MANUFACTURE a new invention which is protected for a while by a PATENT. Proprietary medicines are pharmaceuticals which are manufactured by only one COMPANY and protected from COMPETITION by patent.

PROSPECTUS
A document outlining a COMPANY's plans for issuing new securities, including what it intends to do with the MONEY that it raises from the issue. In many countries the contents of prospectuses are laid down by law and are designed to protect investors from misleading information.

PROTECTIONISM
The erecting of TRADE BARRIERS to shelter a domestic MARKET from overseas COMPETITION.

PROVISION
MONEY put aside by a BUSINESS out of current PROFIT to meet future liabilities. Specific provisions are set aside against liabilities that can be forecast with a degree of certainty. General provisions are set aside against unexpected liabilities.

PROXY
A right to vote that has been delegated to someone else, especially the rights of absentee shareholders at COMPANY meetings that have been delegated to someone who attends the MEETING.

PROXY FIGHT
A struggle between two sets of opposing shareholders to collect the proxies of other shareholders in order to pass a RESOLUTION at a COMPANY MEETING; for example, a resolution that their candidate be elected to the board.

Psychometric testing
The use of tests which claim to measure characteristics of an individual's personality in order to ascertain whether that individual is suitable for a particular job. It includes the use of graphology.

Public company
A COMPANY whose shares can be bought and sold by the public (usually on a recognised STOCK EXCHANGE). The opposite of a PRIVATE COMPANY. Also known as a publicly held company, but not to be confused with a publicly owned company, which is a company that is owned by a government. To confuse matters further, when a publicly owned company is privatised it becomes a public company.

Public offer
A new ISSUE of securities that is offered to the general public. (See also PLACEMENT.)

Public relations
The job of communicating an ORGANISATION's point of view to a number of different audiences; for example, the press, customers and the government. The more specific job of communicating with investors is called INVESTOR RELATIONS.

Publicity
In general, the attention of the public. Something that companies seek to gain for their new products or for their good behaviour (vis-à-vis the environment, for example). In French, *publicité* means ADVERTISING.

Pump priming
A one-off course of action designed to act as a catalyst for a broader economic consequence. Once a pump has been primed it should run by itself thereafter.

Purchase order
A detailed written request to a SUPPLIER for the delivery of GOODS or SERVICES at a specific PRICE. Once the supplier accepts the terms, the ORDER becomes

a legally binding document.

Purchasing power
The capacity of consumers to purchase GOODS and SERVICES, itself a function of the taxes that they pay, their propensity to save, and their morale.

Purchasing power parity
The EXCHANGE RATE between two currencies based on a comparison of how much it takes in each CURRENCY to buy an identical basket of CONSUMER goods. Commonly abbreviated to PPP.

Put option
An OPTION to sell a fixed number of securities at a specified PRICE within a specified period of time.

Pyramid selling
A method of selling products through layers and layers of agents who are structured like a pyramid. The top layer of agents sells to the next layer and so on. The last layer gets to sell to the general public. In practice, the last layer more frequently gets left with a load of unsellable stuff.

QUALIFIED ACCOUNTS
A set of ACCOUNTS to which auditors have added a qualification saying that for one reason or another they are unable to verify all the figures. The reason may be that the COMPANY is involved in a long-running and still unresolved lawsuit, or that it is unable to verify the existence of INVENTORY in a faraway place.

QUALITATIVE RESEARCH
MARKET RESEARCH designed to gain unquantifiable insights into consumers' attitudes and perceptions. It relies heavily on group discussions and in-depth interviews.

If there's a way to do it better ... find it.
Thomas Edison

QUALITY MANAGEMENT
A system developed in Japan after the second world war in which companies aim to improve the quality of everything they do, marginally but continuously. Well expressed in a saying from the Middle East: "Drop by drop we make a lake." (See also TQM.)

Quality is remembered long after
the price is forgotten.
Gucci slogan

QUALITY CIRCLE
A group of employees who get together to consider the quality of their work and how they can improve it. Quality circles rely heavily on charting measurable elements of performance and then rewarding any improvement in those elements.

QUALITY CONTROL
The systematic checking of samples of mass-produced GOODS at various stages in the production PROCESS, but particularly just before the goods are dispatched to the shops. Sometimes abbreviated to QC.

QUANTITATIVE RESEARCH
MARKET RESEARCH that attempts to obtain quantitative findings about a sample of consumers, usually expressed as a percentage: for example, 75% of the sample said that they ate Gozo for breakfast.

QUARTER DAY
The traditional days on which quarterly payments (of rent, and so on) are paid. These vary from country to country.

QUICK RATIO
The ratio of a COMPANY's current assets (CASH, bank accounts, ACCOUNTS PAYABLE) to its current liabilities. The quick ratio gives a rough idea of how well a company could cope with a LIQUIDITY crisis.

QUORUM
The minimum number of people required to be present at an official MEETING, such as a BOARD meeting. If a quorum is not present, any decisions taken by the meeting may be invalid.

QUOTA
A predetermined amount, particularly of GOODS that are allowed to cross TRADE BARRIERS. For example, a country may set a quota for the number of foreign cars that it is prepared to allow across its borders in any one year.

QUOTATION
There are two BUSINESS-related meanings:

- A PRICE that a SUPPLIER "quotes" for the (future) delivery of GOODS or SERVICES.
- What a COMPANY gets when it becomes quoted on a STOCK EXCHANGE – the price at which buyers and sellers are prepared to deal in its shares.

QUOTED COMPANY
A COMPANY whose SHARE PRICE is quoted on a recognised STOCK EXCHANGE.

R&D
Short for research and development, the work that a COMPANY does (and the department that does it) to come up with new products and with new ways of developing existing products.

RACIAL DISCRIMINATION
Discrimination between people on the basis of their race. In most countries racial discrimination in the workplace is illegal.

RALLY
A resurgence of prices (particular of share prices) after a period in which they have been depressed.

RANDOM SAMPLE
A SAMPLE of a population chosen so that (in mathematical theory, at least) every member of that population has an equal chance of being chosen. It is important that samples are random when companies are test-MARKETING new products or doing QUANTITATIVE RESEARCH.

The trouble with the rat race is that even if you win, you're still a rat.
Lily Tomlin, American comedienne

RATE OF INTEREST
The PRICE paid for the use of MONEY over time. This takes into account the rate of INFLATION in an economy, the DEMAND for money in the economy, and the degree of risk to the lender. (See also PRIME RATE.)

RATE OF RETURN
The rate at which FACTORS OF PRODUCTION (land, LABOUR or CAPITAL) produce a RETURN. In analysing a COMPANY'S performance (and comparing it with others) various rates of return are examined; for example, the rate of return on total assets (ROTA), the rate of return on EQUITY (ROE) and the rate of return on capital employed (ROCE).

Rating
The classifying of the characteristics of something according to a scale. It might be a film's suitability for children, a COMPANY's respect for the environment, or the chances of a DEBT being repaid. (See also CREDIT RATING.)

Rationing
The allocation of scarce GOODS or SERVICES by a method other than PRICE. Rationing can be done on a first-come, first-served basis, as when people queue for tickets to an immensely popular concert. Or, as in wartime, it can be done with coupons entitling the holder to a certain amount of goods, and no more. One of the most problematic areas of rationing today is in the provision of health services. How do you decide who is to have their hip replaced next?

Raw materials
The most basic inputs of a manufacturing PROCESS. In many cases these are materials taken from the ground, through mining or agriculture. For steel-making, for example, the raw materials include iron; for carmaking the raw materials include steel.

Real
Corrected for INFLATION. The real PRICE is rarely the same as the NOMINAL price.

Real estate
A North American expression for land and everything that is attached to it.

Real time
Occurring in the present, with special reference to computer systems that take little or no time to perform computations; that is, they carry out instructions almost instantaneously. Really useful in fighter planes.

Recall
There are two meanings:

- A call by a manufacturer for all the products purchased at a particular time to be returned (and a REFUND to be paid). Most frequently used when a PRODUCT is discovered to be faulty.
- The impact of different advertisements measured by the extent to which consumers remember them some time after they were first seen.

RECAPITALISATION
A major reorganisation of the structure of a COMPANY'S CAPITAL, involving, for example, the exchange of shares for loans (or vice versa).

Revitalising General Motors is like teaching an elephant to tap dance. You find the sensitive spots and start poking.

H. Ross Perot, founder of EDS

RECEIPT
A written acknowledgement of payment received for GOODS or SERVICES.

RECEIVABLES
MONEY that has not yet been received by a BUSINESS for bills that it has delivered to its customers. (See also ACCOUNTS RECEIVABLE.)

RECEIVER
Somebody appointed by a court to "receive" a shaky COMPANY's assets on behalf of the company's creditors. Receivers either attempt to help the company to trade itself back into good health, or they liquidate it.

RECESSION
An economy is technically said to be in recession when its GDP has fallen for at least two three-month periods in succession. More generally, a recession is a prolonged period of exceptionally slow economic growth.

Reciprocity
The granting of favours to A by B in return for the same favours being granted to B by A. A common principle underlying countries' negotiations over TRADE and TAX issues.

Recommended retail price
A PRICE which manufacturers recommend that retailers should charge consumers for their products. When recommended retail prices become compulsory they can constitute a RESTRICTIVE PRACTICE. As such, they are illegal in many countries.

Recruitment
The process of identifying and choosing new employees. Specialist recruitment agencies are often called upon to assist in the process.

Recycle
There are two meanings:

- To reuse industrial and commercial waste as the RAW MATERIAL for a new industrial PROCESS; for example, to use waste paper in manufacturing pulp.
- The process whereby banks take in surplus savings in one part of the world and invest them in other places where there is a shortage.

Red clause
A clause typed in red on a LETTER OF CREDIT to indicate that an exporter can receive all the amount due on the letter of credit in advance of shipping the GOODS. Red clauses originated in the Australian wool TRADE.

Red ink
A LOSS. Red ink used to be used by accountants to indicate that a figure was negative.

Redemption
Relating to the time when a financial ASSET matures, as in redemption date or redemption yield.

Redundancy
The loss of a job through no fault of the EMPLOYEE. The job is redundant, (that is, no longer needed) not the employee. Employees who are made redundant are often legally entitled to extra payment as COMPENSATION for losing their jobs. (See also SEVERANCE PAY.)

When the going gets tough, the tough get going.
Kennedy family motto

Re-engineering
A radical redesign of a manufacturing PROCESS. (See also BPR – business process re-engineering.)

Reference
A written statement testifying to the character of someone known to the writer. References are often requested by potential employers from job candidates. (See also TESTIMONIAL)

Refinance
To refund an existing DEBT; borrowing elsewhere to meet a current financial obligation.

Refund
To repay to a CONSUMER the PRICE of GOODS that have been purchased upon the return of the goods and/or the presentation of evidence that they were faulty.

Registered company
A COMPANY that is registered with the authorities of the country in which it is established. In most countries it is illegal to operate as a company without being registered.

Registered office
The address recorded by a COMPANY when it becomes registered, and to which all official communications are sent.

Regulation
The administering of the laws and government rules imposed upon BUSINESS. (See also DEREGULATION.)

Regulator
The person in charge of an agency (or government department) that has been set up for the purpose of regulating a particular INDUSTRY or MARKET.

Reinsurance
The practice among INSURANCE companies of redistributing risk between them. An insurance COMPANY that agrees to insure, say, an oil rig may then buy some reinsurance from another insurer in order to share the risk of the rig sinking.

Relocation
The business of moving elsewhere. This can be the moving elsewhere of a whole COMPANY, or the moving elsewhere of the individuals who work for it.

Remaining maturity
See MATURITY.

Remittance
The sending of money from one person to another, particularly associated with the cross-border payments made by immigrant communities in Europe and North America to the families that they left behind.

Remuneration
The reward for work. Remuneration can be in the form of a SALARY, WAGE, professional FEE, PERK, and so on.

Remuneration committee
The subcommittee of a COMPANY'S BOARD which negotiates and decides on the remuneration of the most senior executives of the company, in particular of the MANAGING DIRECTOR and the other EXECUTIVE directors on the board.

Rent
MONEY paid for the use of REAL ESTATE over time.

Rent control
Government-imposed rules on the amount of RENT that can be charged, designed either to control ruthless landlords or to influence the movement of tenants (for example, out of inner-city areas).

Rent-free period
A period of time in which a TENANT is allowed to occupy PREMISES without paying RENT. Often granted as part of a package to entice a particularly desirable tenant into a new development.

Replacement cost
The COST today of replacing a wasting ASSET. Replacement cost accounting attempts to inject these costs into a COMPANY'S BOOKS.

Replacement demand
The DEMAND for a PRODUCT which arises from consumers wanting to replace old models with new ones. The replacement demand for detergent is high, for cars it is low (and becoming even lower) and for mink coats it is virtually non-existent.

Repositioning
Changing consumers' perception of a PRODUCT or service by altering its packaging or the way in which it is sold.

Restructuring is rather like planting asparagus. You know you should have started three years ago.
Charles Doszher, American industrialist

Reschedule
To alter the MATURITY of a borrower's debts (with the agreement of both the borrower and the lender) in order to facilitate the borrower's chances of repaying on time. Formally putting off until tomorrow what cannot be paid today.

RESEARCH
See MARKET RESEARCH and R&D.

RESERVES
Surplus FUNDS that an ORGANISATION retains for itself and does not distribute to shareholders. Countries also hold reserves. The FOREIGN CURRENCY, gold and facilities with international organisations such as the IMF that they can use if and when they need to intervene in the FOREIGN-EXCHANGE markets to stabilise their currencies. (See HIDDEN RESERVES.)

RESIDENCE
The place where an individual or a COMPANY is said (by a national TAX authority) to reside for the purposes of taxation.

RESIGNATION
The formal ending by an EMPLOYEE of a CONTRACT of employment.

RESOLUTION
The statement of an intent to do something at a COMPANY MEETING. Any meeting's AGENDA consists of a list of resolutions. For example, the AGM will contain resolutions to re-elect the company's auditors, and to receive the directors' report.

RESOURCES
The inputs available to a BUSINESS; in particular, the FACTORS OF PRODUCTION (land, LABOUR and CAPITAL), but also more abstract things such as information and advice. (See also HUMAN RESOURCES.)

RESTRAINT OF TRADE
Any CONTRACT that places a restriction on the way a party to the contract trades. For example, an agreement between an ice-cream manufacturer and a retailer to provide the retailer with refrigerators as long as they are stocked only with the manufacturer's own products.

RESTRICTIVE PRACTICE
A BUSINESS activity that restricts free COMPETITION. In

free-market economies governments keep an eye out for restrictive practices, and clamp down whenever they find them.

Retail
The selling of GOODS and SERVICES to the final CONSUMER.

Retail is detail.
Anon

Retail outlet
Any DISTRIBUTION CHANNEL that sells GOODS and SERVICES RETAIL: a shop, a MAIL-ORDER catalogue, or a WEB SITE.

Retained earnings
That part of a COMPANY'S NET PROFIT which is not distributed as a DIVIDEND.

Retire
There are two BUSINESS-related meanings:

- To end full-time employment, that is, to retire from work.
- To remove the obligation attached to a DEBT, either by early payment or through some other arrangement.

Retirement age
The standard age within a society at which people RETIRE from work. In most developed countries this is between 60 and 65. Someone who retires before the retirement age is said to take early retirement.

Return
What comes back to someone who makes use of land, LABOUR and/or CAPITAL. The return may be in the form of INTEREST (on a LOAN) or a harvest (from agricultural land). A COMPANY'S health can be judged by looking at its return on EQUITY (ROE), its return on ASSETS (ROA) and its return on sales (ROS). (See also SALE OR RETURN.)

Returns
Products which are returned to their SUPPLIER by the purchaser to whom the purchase PRICE is refunded. The term is also used to refer to the responses to a DIRECT MAIL ADVERTISING CAMPAIGN.

Revenue
The INCOME from any commercial activity. Originally, it was the income of the state from taxes (as in Inland Revenue).

Reverse takeover
A TAKEOVER in which the COMPANY being taken over fights back by taking over the company that is trying to buy it.

Revolving credit
A LOAN which permits the borrower to borrow up to a set limit, again and again. The borrower with a revolving credit can borrow up to its limit, repay some of it, and then borrow up to the limit again.

Rights issue
An ISSUE of shares which gives existing shareholders the right to buy the issue at a favourable PRICE and within a specified period of time. Rights that are not taken up can usually be sold on the open MARKET before they expire. In most markets a PUBLIC COMPANY has to make all new share issues in this way in order to prevent existing shareholders from involuntarily having their holdings diluted.

Risk
The chances of losing money. Investors who buy financial instruments such as US government bonds, where the risks of not being repaid are minimal, are said to be risk averse. Some risks can be reduced by hedging, others by taking out INSURANCE COVER.

Risk analysis
The systematic analysis and measurement of the RISK of different investments. There are other types of risk associated with an INVESTMENT besides the

simple one of an inability of the investment to make a RETURN. They include political risk (that a government may compel the borrower to renege on the DEBT) and FOREIGN-EXCHANGE risk (that a debt denominated in another CURRENCY may, through turbulence in the foreign-exchange markets, come to be worth much less by the time it is repaid).

The ultimate risk is not taking a risk.
Sir James Goldsmith

RISK AVERSE
See RISK.

RISK MANAGEMENT
The task of managing the risks that an ORGANISATION takes in the course of its BUSINESS. Ways of reducing RISK include INSURANCE, hedging and disinvestment.

ROBOTICS
The development and use of robots to undertake activity formerly done by humans. In the car INDUSTRY, in particular, robots have taken over many of the manufacturing processes.

ROLL OVER
To extend the MATURITY of a LOAN beyond its original repayment date. In some cases this may involve replacing an old loan with a new one.

RO-RO
A ship where vehicles roll on and then roll off; that is, the vehicles are driven down ramps and straight into the hold of the boat, and likewise in reverse when disembarking.

ROUND
A set of negotiations under the terms of the GATT, such as the Tokyo Round or the Uruguay Round. The purpose of these rounds is to get the member countries to agree to reduce even further the barriers to TRADE between them.

ROYALTY

Money paid in return for exercising a right under a LICENCE. Thus a publisher pays a royalty to an author for the right to publish his work under a COPYRIGHT licence, and a manufacturer pays a PATENT holder for the right to use the patent in a manufacturing process. Royalties are usually calculated as a percentage of the earnings received from exploitation of the licensed rights, so that the interests of the licensor and licensee are linked by the common desire that sales be maximised.

RUN

An unusually intense DEMAND by customers for the same thing at the same time. For example, a run on a BANK is a simultaneous demand by the bank's depositors to withdraw their money. Other runs, such as the run on turkeys just before Christmas, are less worrying (and more predictable).

S&P

See STANDARD & POOR'S.

SABBATICAL

An extended period of leave taken by an EMPLOYEE, often as a right under the terms of their CONTRACT of employment. University teachers, for instance, are often allowed to take a one-term sabbatical every seven years.

SALARY

Regular payment to an EMPLOYEE for his or her work. A salary is usually paid monthly. A weekly payment is generally called a WAGE.

SALE

There are two meanings:

- Any exchange of GOODS or SERVICES for MONEY, commonly used in the plural. For example: "Last week's sales were extremely poor." (See also TURNOVER.)
- A special reduction in prices designed to stimulate sales of the other kind. Retailers hold these sales in what are for them the quiet periods of the year.

Pile it high, sell it cheap.

Early slogan of Tesco supermarket chain

SALE AND LEASE BACK

See LEASE BACK.

SALE OR RETURN

A type of CONTRACT under which GOODS are supplied to a retailer on the basis that if they are not sold within a given time they can be returned to the supplier without payment. (See also CONSIGNMENT.)

SALES PROMOTION

A special SHORT-TERM effort used to promote or LAUNCH a PRODUCT or service. To be effective, a sales promotion needs to be conspicuous and noticed, and it needs to bring in more REVENUE than it costs.

He who has a thing to sell
And goes and whispers in a well
Is not so apt to get the dollars
As he who climbs a tree and hollers.
Anon

SALES QUOTA
A target given by a COMPANY to its sales STAFF setting the volume or VALUE of sales that they are expected to achieve within a given period.

SALES TAX
Any TAX based on the volume or VALUE of sales.

SALESMAN
A person whose main job is to sell GOODS or SERVICES. The word has come to symbolise the slick entrepreneur trying to pass on low products for high prices.

A salesman has got to dream, boy.
It comes with the territory.
Arthur Miller, *Death of a Salesman*

SAMPLE
There are three BUSINESS-related meanings:

- A number of items chosen from all those that exist. Samples are used to test the characteristics of the group as a whole.
- A PRODUCT that is taken as a model for the subsequent MASS PRODUCTION of that product; particularly common in the rag TRADE.
- A small example of a product that is given away to consumers to persuade them to buy it in larger quantities.

SANCTION
An obstruction placed on a country's ability to TRADE freely. Sanctions are usually imposed as a penalty for behaviour disapproved of by the international community; for example, the sanctions imposed on South Africa for its policy of apartheid. Confusingly, the word sanction (as a verb) means to authorise. Hence South Africa sanctioned the policy (of apartheid) that brought about sanctions.

SATURATE
To have such a generous supply of products in a MARKET that it is difficult for a new entrant to gain a foothold.

SCAN
To read electronically the BAR CODE on the packaging of products in a RETAIL OUTLET.

SCENARIO PLANNING
A method of planning for the future that involves getting an ORGANISATION's executives to focus on the changes that they think will be the most significant for their BUSINESS in the future. They are then asked to imagine what such changes might lead to.

You can trust a crystal ball about as far as you can throw it.
Faith Popcorn, American futurologist

SCRAP
An ASSET that is no longer of economic VALUE to an ORGANISATION. But this does not mean that it is of no value to anyone. Scrap can be sold and its value is called the scrap (or salvage) value.

SCRIP ISSUE
A free DISTRIBUTION of shares to a COMPANY's existing shareholders in proportion to their shareholding. A scrip issue is little more than an accounting device; it does nothing to increase the VALUE of the

company or of any shareholder's stake in it. Also known as a bonus issue.

Sealed bid
A BID for a CONTRACT that is presented in a sealed envelope. Nobody knows the details until the envelopes of all bidders for the contract have been handed in. They are then all opened at the same (prearranged) time, and the winning bid is announced.

Search engine
A software PROGRAM that enables a computer to search its DATABASE and retrieve all references to a specified KEYWORD.

Seasonally adjusted
The adjustment of statistics to take account of the fact that BUSINESS activity varies with the seasons; for example, sales figures are distorted during the Christmas and summer holiday periods. Seasonally adjusted data remove the exceptional influence and show the underlying trend.

Secondary market
A MARKET in GOODS or SERVICES which have already been sold to a CONSUMER at least once (especially markets in financial instruments such as bonds and shares).

Secondary picketing
See PICKETING.

Secondment
A temporary job taken by an employee with an ORGANISATION other than the one with which they have a CONTRACT of employment. For example: "He normally works for Rolls-Royce, but he is on secondment this year to the Ministry of Defence."

Secretary
A person who does the formal correspondence required by either an individual or an ORGANISATION. Hence a COMPANY SECRETARY is responsible for

all the official correspondence between the COMPANY and the government or regulator. Company secretaries may also have personal secretaries who type their letters for them. From the French word *secrétaire,* meaning a writing table with drawers in which to keep paper and pens.

SECTOR
A GROUP of companies with some sort of commercial activity in common. The transport sector, for instance, comprises companies involved in transport (airlines, train operators, and so on). The airline companies alone constitute the airline sector.

SECURED LOAN
Any LOAN which gives the lender the right to take possession of assets belonging to the borrower should the loan not be repaid on schedule.

SECURITY
There are two BUSINESS-related meanings:

- Something which is pledged by a borrower to a lender as COLLATERAL for a LOAN. Should the loan not be repaid, the lender has the right to take the security in place of the repayment. The security for a MORTGAGE is the property that has been purchased with the mortgage loan.
- A document which demonstrates its holder's right to a SHARE in a company's EQUITY or to the ownership of one of its bonds. In this sense the word is generally used in the plural (that is, securities).

SEED MONEY
The first (small) investment in a project. Seed money is usually designed to enable the project's backers to prepare a BUSINESS PLAN and to do enough MARKET RESEARCH to persuade a sizeable FINANCIAL INSTITUTION to back the project more fully.

SEGMENTATION
The breaking up of a MARKET according to the characteristics of its consumers. This enables a PRODUCT to be sold in different ways to different segments of its market. Selling pensions to university students requires a dramatically different approach from the way in which they are sold to middle-aged managers.

SELF-EMPLOYED
Someone who works for themselves and is not employed by an ORGANISATION. Self-employed people have to handle their own TAX affairs and have no PERKS.

SELF-REGULATION
The REGULATION of an INDUSTRY done by the industry itself, as opposed to the regulation that is done by government. Industries have an interest in regulating themselves to ensure that no rogue in their midst blackens the reputation of all of them. Most of them prefer to set the rules by which they are judged themselves rather than have the government do it.

SELLER'S MARKET
A MARKET in which DEMAND outstrips supply and in which sellers can get rid of as much PRODUCT as they can lay their hands on.

SEM FABRICA
Spanish for "without a FACTORY", an expression used widely in Latin America to describe elderly entrepreneurs who have sold their businesses and are now living comfortably on the proceeds.

SEMICONDUCTOR
A semi-efficient conductor of electricity, something that conducts less well than metal but better than an insulator (such as rubber). Semiconductors such as silicon are the bedrock of the computer INDUSTRY.

SENIOR DEBT
A LOAN which has first call on a COMPANY's assets in the event of a LIQUIDATION of the COMPANY. A SECURED LOAN is senior DEBT; an unsecured loan is known as junior debt.

SENSITIVITY ANALYSIS
Calculation of the extent to which one BUSINESS variable is affected by changes in another. For instance, calculating the percentage increase in sales for each 1% reduction in the PRICE of a PRODUCT.

SERVICE ECONOMY
An economy in which service industries (those which supply SERVICES rather than FINISHED GOODS or RAW MATERIALS) predominate. Most rich countries are service economies today.

SERVICES
Non-tangible benefits supplied by businesses to consumers. Airplanes are products; flights on airplanes are services.

SET-OFF
The attempt by one party to a CONTRACT to reduce its obligations under the contract by the amount of a counter-obligation arising elsewhere. Thus if A owes B $1m for one deal and B owes A $100,000 for a completely different deal, A might pay B $900,000 and call it quits. But what if B does not acknowledge the debt to A?

SEVERAL LIABILITY
The LIABILITY of a group of people for which they can only be sued individually, and then only for that part of the overall liability incurred by each of them. Several liability thus creates several liabilities. (See also JOINT LIABILITY and JOINT AND SEVERAL LIABILITY.

SEVERANCE PAY
An amount of MONEY to which employees are contractually entitled if their employment is brought

to a premature end through no fault of their own. Severance pay is often related to the individual EMPLOYEE'S length of service with the EMPLOYER.

SEXUAL DISCRIMINATION
Discrimination against someone on the basis of their sex. In many countries sexual discrimination in the workplace is illegal. Nonetheless, the vast majority of people running businesses today are, as they always were, men. (See also GLASS CEILING.)

A woman is like a teabag. Only when she's in hot water do you realise how strong she is.
Anon

SEXUAL HARASSMENT
Unwelcome verbal or physical sexual advances. Sexual harassment in the workplace may be interpreted by the courts as illegal DISCRIMINATION.

SHADOW DIRECTOR
A person who is not a DIRECTOR of a COMPANY but under whose shadow the official directors operate. Shadow directors are often the founders of companies which have gone public. They have been removed from the BOARD, but they still manage to exert considerable influence over it.

SHARE
A portion of something, in particular of the EQUITY of a COMPANY. (See also A AND B SHARES, DEFERRED SHARE, GOLDEN SHARE, MARKET SHARE, NON-VOTING SHARE, ORDINARY SHARE and PREFERENCE SHARE.)

SHARE CERTIFICATE
Documentary evidence of the holder's ownership of a SHARE in the EQUITY of a COMPANY.

SHARE INDEX
An INDEX, such as the FTSE 100, of the prices of leading shares quoted on a particular STOCKMARKET. Their PRICE movements act as a proxy for the market as a whole. (See FTSE 100.)

SHARE OPTION
An option to purchase shares at a given PRICE and within a specified period of time. Share options are frequently offered to senior managers as part of their REMUNERATION packages. The prices at which the options can be exercised ensure that the managers make a sizeable CAPITAL GAIN if the COMPANY performs well while they are running it.

SHARE PREMIUM
The amount of MONEY that a COMPANY raises from a SHARE ISSUE that is in excess of the NOMINAL VALUE of the shares.

SHAREHOLDER
A person or ORGANISATION who owns a SHARE in a COMPANY.

SHAREHOLDERS' FUNDS
The total VALUE of the shareholders' STAKE in their COMPANY. Shareholders' funds are equivalent to the company's CAPITAL and RESERVES. Virtually the same as NET WORTH.

SHELF LIFE
The amount of time that a PRODUCT can be left on the shelf in a RETAIL OUTLET and still be in a fit condition for consumption. The expression is used particularly with respect to foodstuffs.

SHELL COMPANY
A COMPANY that has no significant assets. Its purpose is to act either as a vehicle for legitimate borrowing, or as a way to LAUNDER MONEY and/or keep it out of the eyes of the taxman. Shell companies also provide a way for businesses to get a listing on a STOCK EXCHANGE without having to go through the LISTING procedure.

SHIFT
A number of employees who work together for a fixed period of time. For example: "Today she's working on the night shift." Shift work occurs in manufacturing industries where equipment needs

to be kept running for 24 hours a day, either because demand is exceptionally high or because it is expensive to shut the equipment down and restart it.

SHIPPING AGENT
An AGENT who handles the shipping of GOODS and RAW MATERIALS for a manufacturer. In this context, the word shipping covers all forms of transport, not just ships.

SHIP'S MANIFEST
A list, kept by a ship's captain, of all the different cargo carried on his ship.

SHOP FLOOR
The physical location of a COMPANY's manufacturing processes; also the complete set of all such places. For example: "He was a shop-floor worker until he got promoted to head OFFICE."

SHOP FRONT
The most visible evidence of an ORGANISATION'S existence. For example: "The company's OFFICE in Manhattan is just a shop front. The real BUSINESS goes on in Milwaukee."

SHOP STEWARD
The appointed representative of a TRADE UNION. Each significant BUSINESS unit where a union is represented has its own shop steward. He or she acts as an intermediary between the union and the workers on the SHOP FLOOR.

SHORT
An INVESTOR is said to be short in a STOCK when his supply of it plus his commitments to buy it in the future amount to less than his commitments to sell it in the future. (See also LONG.)

SHORT-TERM
A period of time of 12 months or less. In accounting, a LIABILITY is short-term if it is going to arise within the current ACCOUNTING PERIOD, that is, in

less than 12 months. A short-term LOAN is one with a MATURITY of 12 months or less.

SHORTFALL
The amount by which an actual figure falls short of a targeted figure. For example: "The shortfall on the six-months PROFIT figure was greater than expected."

SHRINKAGE
Any STOCK in a RETAIL OUTLET that is not exchanged for CASH. Shrinkage may occur through theft, damage, or shoddy workmanship. (See also RETURNS.)

SHUTDOWN
The closing down of a sizeable manufacturing operation because:

- there is a shortage of orders;
- the equipment needs retooling; or
- the workers have gone on STRIKE.

SIC
Short for Standard Industrial Classification, a widely used system for classifying industrial products. It is based on a six-digit number in which the first two digits identify a broad INDUSTRY SECTOR, the second two define the sector more narrowly, and the third two define the individual PRODUCT.

SIGHT
If something is payable on sight it means that it is payable on demand. A sight DEPOSIT, for example, is a deposit at a BANK that the depositor can withdraw immediately and at any time.

SIGHT DRAFT
See BANK DRAFT.

SILENT PARTNER
See LIMITED PARTNER and SLEEPING PARTNER.

SILICON VALLEY
Popular name for the valley running between San

Jose and San Francisco in California where many pioneering computer companies grew up. The computer INDUSTRY relies heavily on silicon as a SEMICONDUCTOR.

SIMULATION
An attempt to represent aspects of the real world (economic aspects in particular) by means of mathematical models. Simulation is heavily dependent on the use of advanced computer programs.

SINKING FUND
A FUND into which MONEY is transferred at regular intervals to meet an expected future LIABILITY.

SKILL
Proficiency at a particular task. A skilled WORKFORCE is one whose members have special expertise at something or other. An unskilled workforce consists of people who have had no TRAINING or relevant experience since leaving school.

SLEEPING PARTNER
A partner in a BUSINESS who is not involved in the day-to-day running of the business. Although the expression originally applied only to individuals who worked in a PARTNERSHIP, now it applies to all forms of business, with the word partner being used loosely.

SLOGAN
A memorable phrase or sentence about a PRODUCT that helps to keep the product in consumers' minds.

It may be December outside,
But it's always August under your armpits.
Slogan for an American deodorant

SLUMP
A severe economic RECESSION that falls short of a DEPRESSION. A slump in sales is a short sharp drop in TURNOVER.

SMART
Any PRODUCT with some sort of embedded electronic intelligence is described as smart. A smart card is a CREDIT CARD with an embedded microchip that enables it to manage a CREDIT FACILITY. Smart refrigerators would tell the milkman when you were running out of milk.

SME
Short for small and medium-sized enterprises. In Europe it has become a general term for all small businesses. The SME SECTOR is universally recognised as having special needs. Although it is innovative and nimble, it is hampered by not having access to ECONOMIES OF SCALE.

Small firms have smaller firms upon their backs to bite 'em,
And smaller firms have smaller firms, and so ad infinitum.

Harold Wilson, a former UK prime minister

SOAP
A serialised television drama that (originally) was sponsored by a single company for ADVERTISING purposes. The first soaps were sponsored by soap manufacturers.

SOCIÉTÉ ANONYME
The French equivalent of a limited COMPANY, an indication to the general public that a company enjoys the benefit of LIMITED LIABILITY. Usually abbreviated to SA.

SOFT
A COMMODITY that is soft to the touch, such as sugar or pork bellies, as opposed to silver or platinum.

SOFT CURRENCY
A CURRENCY that is expected to depreciate in VALUE against other currencies. The opposite of HARD CURRENCY.

Soft loan
A loan that is granted on terms that are more generous to the borrower than those that could be obtained in the open market.

Soft market
A market in which supply exceeds demand; one that favours buyers (who hold off in expectation of the price falling) rather than sellers.

Soft sell
A gentle attempt to sell something to a consumer, making no effort to hurry the consumer into making a decision. The opposite of a hard sell.

Software
The electronic programs inside a computer's hardware that enable it to carry out different tasks.

Sogo shosha
The unique trading companies that sit at the heart of all Japanese *zaibatsu*. Their role is to act as the group's agent in all its trading activities. They also serve as an intelligence-gathering operation for the group.

SOHO
The acronym for small office, home office, a recently identified industrial sector consisting of home workers and of people who work in organisations with one or two others. SOHO is a dynamic, fast-growing sector.

Sold as seen
When something being sold comes with no assurances at all from the seller. The buyer must beware – or *caveat emptor*.

Sole trader
A business that is not incorporated and that is run by its owner. The sole owner of the business has sole unlimited liability.

SOLVENT
Having the ability to pay debts as and when they become due. The opposite of INSOLVENT.

SOURCES AND USES OF FUNDS
An accounting statement that shows all the CASH that came in and out of a BUSINESS during a fixed period (usually a year). In some countries such statements are required by law to be submitted as an integral part of the company's annual ACCOUNTS.

SOVEREIGN RISK
The RISK that a country will not pay its obligations as and when they fall due for political, military or economic reasons.

SPAN OF CONTROL
The extent of an individual manager's responsibility, as measured (usually) by the number of people reporting to him. Some argue that this should be no more than six; others think that 20 is not too many.

SPECIAL PROMOTION
A special PROMOTION.

SPECIAL RESOLUTION
A RESOLUTION proposed at a COMPANY MEETING that falls outside the company's normal BUSINESS. For instance, a resolution that a DIRECTOR charged with FRAUD should stand down from the BOARD would be a special resolution.

SPECIALISATION
The process of focusing on a narrow range of things. Specialisation by a COMPANY involves it in manufacturing a smaller and smaller PRODUCT range, or in focusing on one narrow aspect of the manufacturing PROCESS. In the case of an individual, specialisation means concentrating on a narrower range of skills, and mastering them to a greater degree.

SPECIFIC PROVISIONS
See PROVISIONS.

SPECIFICATION
The detailed description of what a CUSTOMER wants done (and, sometimes, of the way in which it is to be done) that is given to a SUPPLIER; for example, to the printer of this book. The supplier then quotes a PRICE on the basis of the "spec".

SPECULATOR
Someone who buys something with the aim of making a quick (and substantial) PROFIT from selling it soon after. In particular, investors in the STOCKMARKET whose interest is in making a quick turn, not in owning corporate assets.

SPIN-OFF
A corporate DIVISION or SUBSIDIARY that is established as a separate corporate entity. Traditionally, the shares in a spin-off are allocated pro-rata to the shareholders of the parent company out of which it has been spun.

SPLIT
See STOCK SPLIT.

SPLIT COMMISSION
The sharing of a COMMISSION between an AGENT who carries out a particular piece of BUSINESS (a BROKER who handles a STOCK transaction, for instance) and the person who introduced the business to the agent.

SPLIT SHIFT
A SHIFT that is broken up into two spells of work separated by a period of time for which the worker is unpaid. Split shifts are suitable for school bus drivers, for example. They need to work in the morning when children go to school and in the afternoon when they come back, but not in between.

Spokesman
A person who speaks on behalf of a COMPANY, or on behalf of its products. Usually someone is employed specially for the task, a person skilled in making muck smell of musk. Occasionally, well-known personalities are adopted to act as spokesmen, such as fashion models and athletes.

Sponsor
There are two BUSINESS-related meanings:

- A big INVESTOR whose declared support for a particular ISSUE of securities encourages others to buy the securities.
- The subsidising of an event by a COMPANY for the purposes of ADVERTISING. The event may be sporting (as in the Whitbread round-the-world yacht race) or it may be a television programme (see SOAP).

Spot check
An unannounced random check to see if work is being done correctly. Spot checks can be used as part of a programme of QUALITY CONTROL.

Spot market
A MARKET in which the prices quoted for GOODS and SERVICES are for immediate payment and for immediate delivery. The original COMMODITY and CURRENCY markets are examples of spot markets.

Spot price
The PRICE of something if it is bought on the spot, and for CASH.

Spread
The difference between one item and another, most frequently the difference between a buying PRICE and a selling price. A bid-offer spread, for example, is the difference between the price that a buyer is prepared to BID for a SECURITY and the price for which a seller is prepared to OFFER the same security.

Spreadsheet
A computer PROGRAM consisting of the relationships between a number of mathematical variables (like prices and costs). A change in one of the variables can be fed into the PROGRAM and its effect on all the others calculated immediately.

Squeeze
A time when the supply of something is scarce. In particular, the supply of MONEY, which leads to a CREDIT squeeze.

Staff
In general, the employees of an ORGANISATION. The origins of the word lie in military history when staff carried out the centralised administrative functions and the line consisted of the troops who actually engaged in battle.

Stag
An INVESTOR who speculates that a new ISSUE of securities will be oversubscribed. Stags buy more securities than they really want in the belief that the heavy DEMAND will cause the ISSUE'S SHARE PRICE to rise sharply as soon as it starts trading.

Stake
Any substantial holding of shares in a COMPANY. The term comes from pioneering farmers who would put stakes in the ground around land that they laid claim to. But see below.

Stakeholder
Anyone who has a "stake" in a company, including employees, suppliers and customers as well as shareholders. Some spread the stakeholder net even wider to include the local community.

Stamp duty
A TAX whose payment is acknowledged by the affixing of stamps to an official document.

Stand-alone
A business PROCESS, or a computer WORKSTATION,

that is independent of any other. In other words, a computer that is not networked to others, or a production process that is not dependent on inputs from elsewhere within the ORGANISATION of which it is a part.

STAND-BY FACILITY

A LOAN that is available to a borrower for a certain period of time if certain conditions are met. In particular, a loan from the IMF to a member country which is made available, usually for up to three years, for as long as the country meets certain economic and financial criteria.

STANDARD

A measure of something that acts as the basis for judging other things of the same type. For example, the time that it takes a car to accelerate from stationary to 60mph is a standard measure of acceleration.

STANDARD DEVIATION

A statistical measure of the extent to which a SAMPLE of data spreads out from a central core figure (usually the average of the sample). The extent, for example, to which daily sales figures for cornflakes deviate from the average daily figure.

STANDARD & POOR'S

One of the world's most influential CREDIT-RATING AGENCIES.

STANDARDISATION

The process of reducing variety in manufacturing or SERVICES to gain economic benefit. The term refers in particular to the process of introducing common specifications for the production of equipment, especially electronic equipment, so that consumers can use any type of SOFTWARE on any type of HARDWARE.

STANDING ORDER

An instruction to a FINANCIAL INSTITUTION to make a fixed payment to a named CREDITOR at regular intervals, usually monthly.

START-UP
A BUSINESS that is just beginning. Its start-up COST is the MONEY that it needed for it to open its doors: to install telephones, to buy equipment and to hire STAFF.

STATEMENT
A written summary of financial transactions. They may be transactions that take place in and out of a BANK ACCOUNT over a given period, or they may be the transactions carried out by a corporation during a given period.

STATUTORY AUDIT
The AUDIT of a BUSINESS that is required by the laws of the country in which the business is registered.

STATUTORY NOTICE
The amount of time decreed by law that must be allowed to pass between the announcement of an intention to end a CONTRACT and the actual ending of the contract. (See also NOTICE.)

STEWARD
Originally, a person who managed the domestic affairs of a family, looking after their estates and so on. Hence a person who manages a BUSINESS on behalf of its owners, or one who manages the affairs of passengers on trains, boats or planes. A company's DIRECTORS can be said to be stewards of the company on behalf of its shareholders. (See also SHOP STEWARD.)

STOCK
There are two meanings:

- The stock of CAPITAL belonging to a COMPANY, which is usually divided up into shares. In the United States the words stocks and shares are virtually interchangeable.
- Another word, preferred by the British, for INVENTORY.

Stock control
The process of managing a COMPANY'S STOCK (or INVENTORY) in the most COST-EFFECTIVE way.

Stock exchange
A place where securities are traded.

Stock option
Another term for SHARE OPTION.

Stock split
The dividing up of a COMPANY'S shares into a larger number. Each SHAREHOLDER in, for example, a three-for-one split gets three shares for each one that they hold. Each of the new shares is worth one-third of the old one. No new VALUE is created. A stock split makes shares with a high denomination more marketable. It is easier to sell three $35 shares than one $105 share.

Stockbroker
A person or FIRM that acts as an AGENT for investors in buying and selling securities on a STOCK EXCHANGE.

Stockmarket
An organised MARKET in financial instruments which signify the ownership of CAPITAL – that is, in bonds, stocks and shares.

Stockpile
To hold on to unnecessarily large quantities of something in order to benefit later from PRICE changes or from shortages of supply.

Stockroom
The place where an ORGANISATION stores its INVENTORY.

Stocks and shares
See STOCK and SHARE.

Straight line
The DEPRECIATION of an ASSET by an equal amount

each year over the full economic life of the asset. (See also DECLINING BALANCE.)

STRATEGIC ALLIANCE
An ALLIANCE formed between two or more organisations with a specific STRATEGIC GOAL in mind.

STRATEGIC GOAL
The aim of a STRATEGY.

STRATEGIC PLANNING
The process of drawing up a STRATEGY. (See also PLANNING.)

STRATEGY
A policy designed to achieve a number of specific objectives. The term originates from a Greek word meaning generalship, the art of mastering the battlefield.

STRESS
The pressure on individuals to perform. Stress in the right amount is essential to good performance, on the sports field as much as in the boardroom. Too much stress, however, causes physical illness and ABSENTEEISM.

STRIKE
The deliberate withholding of their LABOUR by a group of workers as a means of persuading an ORGANISATION to take a particular course of action. The action usually involves an increase in their wages or an improvement in their working conditions.

STRIKE PRICE
The PRICE at which an OPTION states that a SECURITY can be bought or sold in the future.

STRIP
The process of separating (for trading purposes) the INTEREST payments due on a BOND from the CAPITAL payments. Bonds that have been so separated are called strips, an ACRONYM for Separate Trading

of the Registered Interest and Principal of Securities.

STRUCTURE
Any building; and hence the way in which an ORGANISATION builds its lines of command and communication among its various employees.

STYLE
The intangible qualities of an ORGANISATION which uniquely differentiate the way in which it does things. The style of an organisation remains the same even when all its employees change.

SUBCONTRACTOR
Any individual or FIRM to whom a person who has a CONTRACT to do a piece of work passes on some of that work. A subcontractor remains legally responsible for the work being done according to the original contract.

SUBLEASE
A CONTRACT to lease something from someone who is already LEASING it from someone else.

SUBLIMINAL ADVERTISING
The presentation of ADVERTISING in such a way that the recipient is not aware that it has been presented, as, for instance, on a single frame of a film. Subliminal advertising was once considered to be dangerously subversive and was made illegal in the United States. Nowadays most people are sceptical about its effects.

SUBORDINATE DEBT
Any DEBT that can be settled only after other debts have been paid. Such a debt is subordinate (or junior) to the other (senior) debt. (See also SENIOR DEBT.)

SUBSCRIPTION PRICE
There are two BUSINESS-related meanings:

- The COST of buying products or SERVICES that are to be supplied at regular intervals in the future, commonly newspapers or magazines. Subscriptions are usually sold at a large DISCOUNT to the FACE VALUE of the products.

- The PRICE at which a new issue of securities is offered to existing shareholders in a RIGHTS ISSUE.

SUBSIDIARY

A COMPANY that is more than 50% owned and controlled by another company. (See also PARENT COMPANY.)

SUBSIDY

An economic benefit bestowed on a group of individuals or corporations by a government to encourage a particular form of economic behaviour. Governments often give subsidies to their country's exporters and to companies that invest in under-developed regions.

SUCCESSION PLANNING

The process of preparing for another person to succeed the incumbent in a senior POSITION. It has been suggested, rather extremely, that succession planning is the most important task of any CEO. Succession planning has traditionally proved to be particularly difficult in a FAMILY FIRM.

It is not enough to succeed. Others must fail.

Maurice Saatchi, joint founder of
Saatchi & Saatchi advertising agency

SUGGESTIONS BOX

A sealed place where the employees of an ORGANISATION can put suggestions (anonymously if they wish) about ways in which the organisation can be improved.

SUNRISE INDUSTRY

An INDUSTRY that is at the beginning of its economic life and is growing fast. Such industries today would include biotechnology and electronic commerce.

SUNSET INDUSTRY
An INDUSTRY that is near the end of its economic life, such as the car-phone industry, which is being made extinct by the spread of mobile phones.

SUPERMARKET
A large high-volume self-service shop. Supermarkets have come to dominate the grocery TRADE in most developed countries.

SUPERVISORY BOARD
A second BOARD required in certain countries, such as Germany. The supervisory board consists of a number of NON-EXECUTIVE DIRECTORS and is charged with keeping an eye on the MANAGEMENT board (which consists of EXECUTIVE DIRECTORS). In particular, it watches to see that the interests of shareholders and creditors are not compromised in management's pursuit of its own interests.

SUPPLIER
Someone who supplies an ORGANISATION with needed GOODS or SERVICES. (See also PREFERRED SUPPLIER.)

SUPPLIER CREDIT
A LOAN to an exporter enabling it to finance an ORDER from a buyer in another country. The loan may be guaranteed by the EXPORT CREDIT agency of the exporting COMPANY's country.

SUPPLY
The other fundamental concept in ECONOMICS (see also DEMAND). The extent to which producers are prepared to MANUFACTURE GOODS and SERVICES at different prices.

SUPPLY CHAIN
The flow of materials in and out of an ORGANISATION, their movement through the organisation during the production PROCESS, and their final delivery (as a PRODUCT) to a POINT OF SALE.

SUSPENSE ACCOUNT
A BANK ACCOUNT that is set up to hold FUNDS temporarily until they can be transferred to their rightful home. Their rightful ownership may be in question, or the funds may be arriving in small amounts that are being collected until they can be transferred more economically as a single item.

SUSPENSION
Disciplinary action taken against an EMPLOYEE that falls short of DISMISSAL. Suspension involves the employee in not turning up to work for a while, usually without pay.

SUSTAINABLE DEVELOPMENT
Economic development that does not exhaust in the short term those resources that will enable the development to continue in the long term.

SWAP
A transaction in which assets change hands without the intermediation of MONEY. The assets may be financial. For example, western central banks have an agreement to swap currencies among themselves should they need to support each other's exchange rates.

SWEATSHOP
A small manufacturing plant in which cheap LABOUR is made to work long hours at exhausting tasks. Sweatshops are associated in particular with the garment INDUSTRY.

SWING PRODUCER
The most dominant member of a CARTEL, and the one which is expected to support the weaker members when they have difficulty in living within the cartel's terms. The swing producer either boosts supply by adding extra production at short notice, or reduces it by withholding production. Within OPEC, the oil-producers' cartel, Saudi Arabia plays the role of swing producer.

SYNDICATE
A GROUP of companies or individuals who get together to carry out an activity that each of them would not be prepared to carry out on their own. Financial institutions, for example, get together to give syndicated loans to borrowers whose financial requirements are far greater than any one of the institutions would be prepared to shoulder alone.

SYNDICAT
The French word for TRADE UNION.

SYNERGY
The idea that companies can make 2 + 2 = 5 by combining operations in imaginative and cost-saving ways. Hence if one computer manufacturer buys another and makes savings by combining OVERHEADS (while keeping the combined sales figure of the two firms constant) it is said to have created synergy.

SYSTEM
The orderly arrangement of parts into a single whole; generally, a single whole that has a single purpose. Hence the human central nervous system is an arrangement of body parts designed to gather and transmit messages to and from the nerves. Likewise, a computer system.

TACTIC
One of a series of SHORT-TERM steps that must be taken to fulfil a longer-term STRATEGY.

TAKE-HOME PAY
The amount of PAY that employees actually take home; that is, their gross pay net of TAX, NATIONAL INSURANCE and other deductions that are made in advance of payment.

TAKEOVER
The formal process whereby one COMPANY buys another. In the case of a QUOTED COMPANY this involves following the often complex rules of the STOCK EXCHANGE on which the company is quoted. (See also HOSTILE TAKEOVER and REVERSE TAKEOVER.)

TANGIBLE ASSET
Literally, an ASSET that can be touched. Buildings, machines and CASH are all tangible assets. (See also INTANGIBLE ASSET.)

TANGIBLE NET WORTH
The NET WORTH of an ORGANISATION minus its intangible assets, things like GOODWILL and the VALUE of patents. Tangible net worth gives a more immediately realisable value of the organisation.

TARGET MARKET
The specific MARKET at which a COMPANY aims its products; for example, teenagers, elderly widows, and so on. The manufacturer of a MASS MARKET PRODUCT does not have a target. It hopes that everybody will buy its MERCHANDISE.

TARIFF
There are two meanings:

- An AD VALOREM TAX imposed on imported GOODS, often as a form of PROTECTIONISM.
- A schedule of prices.

TAX
The dues that are levied on individuals and cor-

porations to pay for the running of governments.

Tax avoidance
The setting up of artificial (but perfectly legal) schemes to reduce the amount of TAX that an individual or COMPANY has to pay to a government. (See also TAX EVASION.)

Tax assessment
A formal agreement between a taxpayer and a government as to how much TAX is due from the taxpayer for a particular period.

Tax deductible
Any EXPENSE which can be paid for out of untaxed INCOME without incurring a TAX LIABILITY.

Tax evasion
The use of illegal means to reduce the amount of TAX due. Someone found guilty of tax evasion may be imprisoned or heavily fined. Contrast with TAX AVOIDANCE.

Tax haven
Any place where the rates of TAX are consistently lower than in the majority of industrialised countries. Tax havens are often hot and small islands.

Tax incentive
Use of the TAX system to encourage or discourage particular forms of economic behaviour. (See also SUBSIDY.)

Tax loss
Any LOSS made by a COMPANY which it is able to transfer to another ACCOUNTING PERIOD and to set off (for TAX purposes) against PROFIT arising during that period.

Tax return
The form on which the details of a taxpayer's INCOME, expenditure and CAPITAL GAINS are sent to the tax authorities.

TAX SHELTER
A (legal) scheme which enables someone to shelter otherwise taxable INCOME from any liability to TAX. In many countries charitable giving and PENSION funds are tax shelters.

TEAM-BUILDING
Techniques for improving the ways in which individuals work together in teams. Team-building aims to make teams more than the sum of their parts.

TEAMWORK
Work that is done in teams. An increasing amount of workplace activity consists of teamwork.

TEASER
A short ADVERTISEMENT that does not name the PRODUCT being advertised, but merely hints at more ADVERTISING to come. Teasers are often used to launch new products.

TECHNOLOGY
The use of science and scientific methods to improve performance. (See also HIGH-TECH.)

TECHNOLOGY TRANSFER
The transfer of a COMPANY's technology in return for access to a MARKET. Technology transfer is frequently promised by western companies as a way of gaining access to developing-country markets.

Teleconferencing is so rational,
it will never succeed.
John Naisbitt, author of *Megatrends*

TELECONFERENCE
A prolonged telephone conversation between more than two people situated in more than two places. Teleconferences are a substitute for meetings in cases where the participants cannot easily get together in the same room at the same time.

TELEMARKETING
The use of the telephone as a channel for MARKETING GOODS and SERVICES.

TELEWORKER
The practice of working at a distance from a head OFFICE or WORKSTATION via MODEM links and telecommunications. (See also HOME WORKER.)

TELEX
An out-of-date method of transmitting typed messages via telephone lines. The telex was largely made redundant by the FAX machine.

TEMP
Someone who is temporarily employed by an ORGANISATION to do a set task, often secretarial, for a short time.

TENANT
Somebody who holds a right to occupy land or buildings that are owned by somebody else.

TENDER
To make an offer (in writing) to do a certain specified piece of work for a specified PRICE.

TENDER OFFER
An OFFER to buy a specified number of securities at a specified PRICE. If fewer than the specified number of securities are offered, the person making the offer is not obliged to buy any of them.

TERM
There are two BUSINESS-related meanings:

- The period of time during which the conditions of a CONTRACT apply.
- The conditions themselves, as in "terms and conditions".

TERM LOAN
Any LOAN which has to be repaid in full within a stated period of time.

Terminal
The interface between a computer NETWORK and an individual computer user.

Terms of trade
The ratio of a country's export prices to its import prices. The prices are calculated as an INDEX based on an arbitrary starting point. Terms of TRADE thus measure changes over time rather than absolute values.

Test market
To try out a new PRODUCT or service by launching it initially in a limited area.

Testimonial
A statement by a respected source vouching for the high quality of a PRODUCT or a person. (See also REFERENCE.)

Third party
Someone invited to play a role in a CONTRACT or agreement who is not one of the two parties to the agreement; an outsider with an independent view.

Time and a half
The payment to an employee of 1.5 times their normal hourly rate for working at an anti-social time outside their normal working hours; in particular, the rate paid in the West for working in the early evening or on Saturdays.

Time and motion
An old-fashioned system of measuring the time taken and the motions required to carry out particular industrial tasks. Time and motion studies were designed as a way of measuring changes in individual employees' PRODUCTIVITY.

Time draft
See BANK DRAFT.

Time management
A systematic way of managing the use of time,

particularly in the workplace, based on the idea that time is MONEY. One popular time-management tool is called a diary.

TITLE

The right to the ownership of property. If someone has "good title" to a property, it means that there is no dispute about their ownership of that property.

TOLL-FREE NUMBER

A telephone number where the receiver pays for the calls rather than the caller. Toll-free numbers are widely used in certain forms of MARKETING.

TQM

Short for total quality management, the idea that QUALITY MANAGEMENT should infuse every single PROCESS in a COMPANY's operations.

TRADE

There are two meanings:

- To buy and sell GOODS and SERVICES, usually across national boundaries.
- A profession or skill. For example: "He's in the meat trade."

TRADE BARRIER

Something that hinders the free flow of TRADE, especially import duties and things which make imported GOODS less competitive vis-à-vis domestically produced goods.

TRADE DISCOUNT

A DISCOUNT given by one member of a TRADE to another; for example, by a wholesaler of garments to the owner of a fashion boutique.

TRADE FAIR

A large organised event at which producers of a defined range of GOODS and SERVICES (often from a number of different countries) show off their wares to potential customers and to each other.

Trademark
The unique mark that a manufacturer puts on to its products to distinguish them from any other manufacturers' products; for example, the label on a pair of Levi jeans. To help protect them from being copied, manufacturers can have their trademarks officially registered in most of the world's leading industrial countries. To enjoy the protection of registration, however, a manufacturer must demonstrate that its mark is both distinctive and in continuous use.

Trade mission
An organised trip abroad by a group of businessmen designed to introduce them to potential customers, representatives, politicians, and so on, in the foreign country.

Trade off
Yielding one ASSET to gain another. For example, selling a building to realise a tax LOSS that can then be set off against the year's trading PROFIT.

Trade secret
Any proprietary way of conducting a TRADE (or profession) that enables its practitioner to be more competitive than its rivals. No FIRM wants its trade secrets to be discovered by anybody else.

Trade union
A group of workers who organise themselves to promote the rights of employees and to improve conditions in the workplace. In particular, a union is able to use the collective bargaining power of all its members when negotiating with employers on matters such as WAGE increases.

Trainee
A person in the process of being trained how to do a particular job. If a trainee fails to pick up the necessary skills within a certain time, he or she may not be taken on by the COMPANY as a full-time EMPLOYEE.

TRAINING
The process of providing employees with the knowledge and/or skills that they need to do their jobs better.

Education costs money,
but then so does ignorance.
Claus Moser

TRANSACTION COST
The COST of carrying out a transaction; for example, the cost of clearing a CHEQUE, or of buying something at an AUCTION.

TRANSFER PAYMENT
A payment by a government to its citizens that is not made as a reward for the supply of GOODS or SERVICES – for example, unemployment benefit.

TRANSFER PRICING
The shifting of PROFIT from one part of a GROUP to another by the charging of artificial (non-MARKET) prices for the provision of GOODS and SERVICES between the parts. Transfer pricing is used to move taxable profits from a high-TAX jurisdiction to a low-tax one.

TRANSNATIONAL
A COMPANY which straddles national boundaries. A transnational company is not a MULTINATIONAL. The latter's business operations work independently of each other. The many different and far-flung operations of a transnational are inextricably linked with each other.

TRANSPARENCY
The principle of making COMPANY ACCOUNTS as clear as possible so that their readers can see for themselves the transactions that underlie them.

TRANSSHIPMENT
The practice of unloading a cargo at one place (a port or an airport, for example) so that it can be

transferred to another mode of transport that will take it on to its final destination.

Traveller's cheque
A means of enabling travellers to make payments when abroad. The traveller's CHEQUE, now over 100 years old, relies on the simple security device of the double signature. Owners sign once when they buy the cheque, and again when they sell it. If they lose the cheque in between signatures they can get it replaced by the issuer.

Treasurer
The (senior) manager within a COMPANY who is responsible for the safekeeping of all the MONEY that comes into the BUSINESS, and for the wise spending of the money that goes out of it.

Trial offer
A special PROMOTION that allows a CONSUMER to try a PRODUCT for a period of time before deciding whether or not to buy it.

Trigger price
The PRICE of imported GOODS below which predetermined restrictions on IMPORTS come into effect. The restrictions are aimed at preventing cheap imports from flooding the MARKET and damaging domestic producers.

Triple A
See AAA.

Troubleshooter
A person who goes into troubled companies at a senior level in order to solve specific SHORT-TERM problems. (See also INTERIM MANAGER.)

True and fair
The accountants' mantra: that the figures in a COMPANY'S ACCOUNTS should represent a true and fair view of the company's affairs. The idea is subject to individual interpretation.

Trust company
A company that is in business to act as a trustee for individuals and other businesses.

Trustee
A person who is entrusted with looking after the property of someone else. This may be the property of a child or of someone who has died.

Trustee in bankruptcy
A person appointed as a trustee by a court in a case of bankruptcy. The trustee in bankruptcy takes title to the bankrupt company's assets while they are being disposed of.

Turnkey project
A large-scale building project where the contractor agrees to see to every detail of the project. The purchaser has only to turn the key when the project is finished in order to take possession.

Turnover
The total amount of money obtained by an organisation for the goods and services that it has sold, less the money that it has paid back for returns.

Two-tier board
Any company board that is divided into two parts; as, for instance, in Germany where public companies have both a management board and a supervisory board.

Tycoon
A successful entrepreneur. Someone with fast cars, pretty girls and big cigars as standard accoutrements, typified by the hero of *The Last Tycoon*, F. Scott Fitzgerald's novel about Hollywood in the 1930s.

Ultra vires
An action that goes beyond the powers of the organisation undertaking it.

UNCTAD
The ACRONYM for United Nations Conference on Trade and Development, an arm of the UN that aims, in particular, to increase TRADE between developing countries and the rest of the world.

Unbundling
The disentangling of businesses within a CONGLOMERATE so that each is run separately as an individual unit.

Undercapitalised
The provision of insufficient CAPITAL for a BUSINESS to operate without financial strain.

Underground economy
Part of an economy that is unrecorded by the TAX authorities. It may be unrecorded because it involves a BARTER transaction, for example, or because it is attempting to evade tax. (See also BLACK ECONOMY.)

Underwrite
There are two meanings:

- To assume the RISK involved in a new ISSUE of securities. The people who do this (usually banks) are called underwriters.
- To take on an INSURANCE risk in return for a PREMIUM.

Unearned income
Any INCOME that is not earned from employment, such as dividends, INTEREST payments and lottery prizes. Some governments treat unearned income differently from earned income for TAX purposes.

Unemployed
People who are not employed but would like to be. The LONG-TERM unemployed are people who

have been unemployed for a continuous period of more than a year.

UNFAIR DISMISSAL
Terminating someone's CONTRACT of employment without good cause. Employees thus dismissed have the right to sue their employers for DAMAGES.

UNFAIR TRADE
TRADE in GOODS that have been subsidised in ways that break the rules of one of the international trading agreements (see NAFTA, ASEAN and GATT).

UNION
See TRADE UNION.

UNIT COST
The COST of producing one unit of a PRODUCT or service.

UNITARY TAX
A revolutionary form of TAX system pioneered by the US state of California. Under a unitary tax system a COMPANY is taxed on a percentage of its worldwide PROFIT rather than on the profit which the company claims arose within the fiscal authority's jurisdiction. The percentage may be based on the share of the company's sales that took place in the jurisdiction.

UNIVERSAL BANK
A BANK that is allowed to carry out a wide range of financial services, almost without limit. In most countries banks are restricted by law as to the sort of services they can offer.

UNLIMITED COMPANY
A COMPANY that does not have the protection of LIMITED LIABILITY. The directors of the company are personally liable for all its obligations, without limit.

UNLISTED SECURITIES MARKET
A MARKET in securities that are not listed on a

recognised STOCK EXCHANGE. Such securities are traded informally, and individual buyers generally have to be matched with sellers. (See also OVER-THE-COUNTER.)

UNQUOTED COMPANY
A COMPANY whose shares are not quoted on a recognised STOCK EXCHANGE. When there is no quoted MARKET PRICE for a company's shares, MARKETING them is not easy.

UPGRADE
To do something that improves the quality or performance of something that already exists; for example, buying more memory for a computer, or improving the CREDIT RATING of a COMPANY'S DEBT.

UPMARKET
A MARKETING term based on a theoretical division of markets into a top, a middle and a bottom. A PRODUCT aimed to appeal to the top end of the MARKET is said to be upmarket. The division of markets can be based on social class, wealth or lifestyle. Contrast with DOWNMARKET.

UPSTREAM
An activity that is close to the original RAW MATERIALS used in a PROCESS (particularly in oil refining). Drilling in the desert, for example, is more upstream than the MANUFACTURE of petrochemicals.

USEFUL LIFE
The length of time during which an ASSET produces more than the cost of its upkeep. An indicator of the period over which the asset should be depreciated.

If you are not thinking customer,
you are not thinking.
Theodore Levitt

USER FRIENDLY
Indicating that something is friendly to a user, that

it is uncomplicated and requires little instruction. The expression originated in the computer INDUSTRY but is now used more widely. For example: "This is a user-friendly guide book."

USER GROUP

A group of consumers who are brought together by a COMPANY'S MARKETING department to examine and discuss their attitudes to the company's products and to those of its rivals. A sophisticated form of MARKET RESEARCH.

USM

Short for UNLISTED SECURITIES MARKET.

USP

Short for unique selling proposition, something a PRODUCT has which differentiates it from all its rivals. Its USP then becomes a central focus of the product's ADVERTISING CAMPAIGN.

If you can't be different,
you might as well be damned.

Roberto Goizueta, former head of Coca-Cola

USURY

The charging of exorbitant rates of INTEREST for loans. Most developed countries now have laws against usury, although CREDIT-CARD companies manage to escape them. In Europe such laws can be traced back to the 15th century.

UTILITY

Any COMPANY that provides SERVICES which are essential to the comfortable running of homes and offices, such as electricity, gas and water.

VALUE
A subjective measure of worth. What something is worth to its owner. Something that is a valuable piece of information to one person may be worthless to the next.

VALUE ADDED
The VALUE that a PROCESS adds to the GOODS and SERVICES it is processing; the amount by which it increases their worth in a MARKET. That is, the PRICE fetched for the output from the process minus the COST of the inputs put into the process.

VALUE CHAIN
The interlinking activities that take place within an ORGANISATION in the PROCESS of converting its inputs into its outputs. Identifying these activities and finding ways to perform them more efficiently is a way for companies to gain COMPETITIVE ADVANTAGE over their rivals.

VARIABLE COST
A COST that varies in line with the volume of production. For example, the cost of steel is a variable cost in the production of automobiles; the cost of heating the FACTORY is not.

VARIABLE RATE
A RATE OF INTEREST which changes in line with some BENCHMARK figure. The extent and frequency with which the rate changes is laid down (for example, no more than once every six months, and then by less than two percentage points). Contrast with FLOATING RATE, which has no limits to its fluctuation.

VAT
Short for value added tax, an AD VALOREM TAX based on the VALUE ADDED to GOODS and SERVICES. VAT is collected all along the production PROCESS, but the burden of paying the tax falls on the final CONSUMER.

VENTURE CAPITAL

MONEY that is put up by a FINANCIAL INSTITUTION or wealthy individual to back a risky project, either in its early stages or when it needs a new injection of CAPITAL. Because of the high RISK involved, venture capital expects a higher RATE OF RETURN than that obtained from normal EQUITY.

For the first four years, no new enterprise produces profits. Even Mozart didn't start writing music until he was four.

Peter Drucker, American business academic

VERGLEICH

Germany's version of CHAPTER 11, a breathing space for companies in financial difficulty. *Ver-gleich* allows them to write off some of their debts if they meet payment terms agreed with their creditors.

VERTICAL INTEGRATION

The integration of businesses whose activities follow each other sequentially. If a garment manufacturer were to buy a spinning mill or a garment shop, it would be an example of vertical integration. Likewise, a food manufacturer that buys a chain of grocers.

VICIOUS CIRCLE

A sequence of events, each of which leads on inevitably to a worse situation, and each of which triggers another such event. Late payment by a CUSTOMER, for instance, might lead to the need for a new BANK LOAN, which might lead to an unfavourable CREDIT RATING, which might lead to ... a vicious circle. Contrast with VIRTUOUS CIRCLE.

VIDEOCONFERENCE

A way of communicating between groups of people in remote places via the telephone and television. A videoconference has the added bonus, compared with a TELECONFERENCE, of allowing the participants to see each other in real time as well as to hear each other.

VIRTUAL
Creating the attributes of something without actually creating the thing itself. A virtual OFFICE, for example, does not exist in an office building. It exists in a travelling SALESMAN's hotel room when he links up his computer to his colleagues' and starts working as if he were in an office. A virtual corporation is a COMPANY with a large TURNOVER, virtually no PREMISES and few STAFF.

VIRTUOUS CIRCLE
A sequence of events which leads from good to better. Each of the events triggers another which improves things even more. Contrast with VICIOUS CIRCLE.

VIRUS
A computer PROGRAM which destroys computer data and other programs. Viruses can be introduced into a computer via any link with the outside world: a floppy DISK, a MODEM link, or a CD.

VISIBLE TRADE
TRADE between countries in manufactured GOODS; things that can be seen, such as cars and computers, rather than INSURANCE policies and room service. (See also INVISIBLES.)

VISION
A lofty and far-seeing aspiration that a COMPANY puts in writing in order to inspire its employees into working for something above and beyond their daily wages.

If you can dream it, you can do it.
Walt Disney

VOICE MAIL
A telephone system which allows each individual within an ORGANISATION to have a phone that can receive recorded messages from incoming callers when individuals are away from their desks. A sort of networked answerphone.

VOICE-OVER
The voice which is added to a filmed ADVERTISEMENT, in a recording studio, after the film has been made.

VOICE RECOGNITION
The ability of an electronic device to distinguish the sound of an individual human voice. Voice-recognition technology has many potential uses, such as accessing BANK accounts and computers.

VOLATILITY
The extent to which something is liable to fluctuate violently and frequently, especially the PRICE of shares, currencies and loans.

VOLUME DISCOUNT
A DISCOUNT given to a buyer that is related to the volume of GOODS that the buyer purchases. For example, if a single item costs $100, but buying ten of the items costs only $900, there is a volume discount of 10%.

VOLUNTARY LIQUIDATION
See LIQUIDATION.

VOTING RIGHTS
Rights enabling the holder of a SHARE in a COMPANY to vote on issues raised at the company's general meetings. (See also PROXY.)

WAGE
The monetary reward for LABOUR.

WAGE FREEZE
The halting (or limiting) by a government of WAGE increases throughout an economy, once a popular way of attempting to control INFLATION.

WALKOUT
An organised stoppage of work by a group of employees in an attempt to obtain improved working conditions and/or wages.

WALL STREET
The street on Manhattan Island where the New York Stock Exchange is situated, a name that has become a synonym for financial markets in general, and for American capitalism in particular.

WAREHOUSE
There are two meanings:

- The physical place where a company stores its STOCK (INVENTORY). Such places are usually on the outskirts of big towns, where property prices are low, but close to arterial transport routes.
- To buy shares in a COMPANY in the names of nominees in order to disguise the fact that a connected group of investors is building up a large STAKE.

WARRANT
A certificate entitling its holder to buy shares in a COMPANY at a future date and at a prescribed PRICE.

WARRANTY
A GUARANTEE given by a seller of GOODS that the goods will perform as promised. Warranties have a finite life and do not cover damage that is not the fault of the manufacturer.

WASTE MANAGEMENT
The systematic management of the waste products

created by an industrial PROCESS; that is, products which are surplus to the process in question. Some waste products can be recycled into different manufacturing processes; others can be used directly as by-products; and others need to be broken down into biodegradable substances.

WASTING ASSET
A FIXED ASSET with a finite USEFUL LIFE, such as a machine that eventually wears out, or a gold mine that is eventually exhausted.

WATCHDOG
An officially appointed body (or person) that watches over the activity of an INDUSTRY to see that it is not, for instance, anti-competitive or in some other way against the public interest.

WAYBILL
A document accompanying a shipment of GOODS that sets out the route that is to be followed by the goods and the cost of the shipment. (See also AIR WAYBILL.)

WEB SITE
An electronic site on the WORLD WIDE WEB where a COMPANY, or an individual, lays out information about itself. Each web site has a unique address. Individuals with access to the INTERNET can key in to that address and gain access to the information on the site.

WHISTLEBLOWER
An EMPLOYEE who alerts the authorities to the fact that his or her EMPLOYER is engaged in illegal activity. Whistleblowers sometimes have special protection under the law.

WHITE COLLAR
A term used to refer to those workers in an ORGANISATION who wear a white collar, that is, a smart shirt and tie rather than a set of overalls. It is a similar distinction to that between STAFF and line workers. (See also BLUE COLLAR.)

WHITE GOODS
Electrical CONSUMER GOODS that are traditionally encased in white enamel, such as refrigerators and washing machines. (See also BROWN GOODS.)

WHITE KNIGHT
An INVESTOR who comes to the rescue of a COMPANY that is subject to a hostile TAKEOVER.

WHOLESALE
The purchasing of large volumes of GOODS direct from manufacturers in order to sell them in smaller volumes to retailers.

WILDCAT STRIKE
A sudden and unofficial STRIKE by a group of employees that is not recognised by the employees' TRADE UNION. A wildcat strike may begin with a WALKOUT.

WINDFALL PROFIT
A sudden and unexpected PROFIT that is not a result of the conscious effort of the beneficiary. For example, the compulsory purchase of waste land by a government for the purposes of road-building might result in a windfall profit for the landowner.

WINDING UP
The process of closing down a COMPANY, selling off its assets and removing it from official records. (See also LIQUIDATION.)

WINDOW DRESSING
The deliberate tarting up of a COMPANY'S ACCOUNTS to make them look as attractive as possible to investors, employees and others. Window dressing need not be illegal. For a number of items that appear in accounts there is no single correct method of valuation.

WINDOW OF OPPORTUNITY
A short period of time in which the conditions for carrying out a particular task are highly

favourable. There may, for example, be a window of opportunity for a COMPANY to issue new shares; a time when the STOCKMARKET is briefly able to fetch a high PRICE for the shares.

WITHHOLDING TAX
A TAX that is withheld at source on INCOME or CAPITAL; that is, before the beneficiary has received the MONEY on which the tax is being levied. PAYE is a withholding tax.

WORD PROCESSOR
A simple sort of computer that carries out the functions of a typewriter, but more quickly.

WORLD WIDE WEB
The computer SOFTWARE that allows a person sitting in front of a PC to gain instantaneous access to electronic information provided by organisations thousands of miles away via the INTERNET. (See also WEB SITE.)

WORK EXPERIENCE
A short posting of a student with a COMPANY that is designed to give the young person experience of full-time work and of a working environment.

WORK IN PROGRESS
All the semi-finished GOODS that exist within a BUSINESS and are on their way towards becoming FINISHED GOODS. Also, the VALUE of all those goods which is shown in the COMPANY'S ACCOUNTS as an ASSET. Referred to in the United States as work in process.

WORK PERMIT
An official permit given by a government to people who are not citizens of that government's country, allowing them to take up formal paid employment within the country.

WORKSTATION
A place within an OFFICE or a home that is equipped with the tools needed to do a particular

job, especially one that requires the use of a computer, MODEM and telephone. A workstation can also be the place where a carpenter does his work.

WORK-TO-RULE
A refusal by employees to do work that falls outside the terms of their CONTRACT, strictly interpreted. This means, for instance, that they refuse to work OVERTIME. The work-to-rule is a common tactic used in industrial disputes.

WORKFORCE
The total of all employees in either an INDUSTRY or an individual COMPANY. The same as labour force.

WORKING CAPITAL
A FIRM'S current assets minus its current liabilities. (See also CURRENT RATIO.)

WORKLOAD
A quantitative measure of the amount of work that an individual is expected to do in a particular job during a fixed period of time.

WRITE DOWN
To reduce the VALUE of an ASSET in the BOOKS of a COMPANY.

WRITE OFF
To reduce to zero the VALUE of an ASSET in the BOOKS of a COMPANY.

WTO
Short for World Trade Organisation, a Geneva-based ORGANISATION that acts as a kind of WATCHDOG for the world's trading system. It oversees the enforcement of the GATT.

YEAR-END
The last day of an ACCOUNTING PERIOD, the day on which the BOOKS are brought to a close. Transactions before that day are taken into account; transactions after it are (by and large) not.

YIELD
The rate of output of any of the FACTORS OF PRODUCTION (that is, of land, LABOUR or CAPITAL). Land yields, for example, are measured by the amount of crop produced per hectare; the yield on SHARE capital is measured by the amount of DIVIDEND paid.

YIELD CURVE
A graph showing the different yields that are obtained from financial instruments of the same quality but of different MATURITY. A yield curve plots the yield of the instruments against their maturity.

ZAIBATSU

Huge industrial conglomerates built up in Japan as the engine of the country's industrial revolution, groups such as Mitsubishi and Sumitomo. Each *zaibatsu* invariably embraces a BANK and a *sogo shosha*. Although disbanded after the second world war, many *zaibatsu* have been reformed since.

ZAP

The practice of using a remote-control device to switch from one television channel to another, particularly to avoid having to watch advertisements. Zapping has a powerful influence on the effectiveness of television ADVERTISING.

ZERO-BASE BUDGETING

A method of drawing up a BUDGET which starts from zero; that is, it assumes that there was no budget at all in previous years. This avoids the trap of slavishly following what was decreed to be a correct figure in a previous period, and then updating it by adding 10%.

ZERO-COUPON BOND

A BOND which does not pay any INTEREST. A zero-coupon bond is sold at a DEEP DISCOUNT to its FACE VALUE. The owner's gain comes from the gradual appreciation of the bond. On MATURITY it will be redeemed at its face value.

ZERO DEFECTS

To have no errors in a product or process – a common aim of TQM.

ZERO-SUM GAME

Any game in which the gains to the winner (or winners) are equal and opposite to the losses of the loser (or losers). Gambling is a zero-sum game; BUSINESS is not. A new entrant to a MARKET can have the effect of increasing the size of the market in such a way that all the participants in it BENEFIT.